EXPLORING PAPIER-MÂCHÉ

BY VICTORIA BEDFORD BETTS

Printed in the United States
Fourth and Revised Edition—1962

DEDICATED

TO TEACHERS—for their patience, understanding and love.

TÓ CHILDREN—for being themselves.

FOREWORD

Primarily, this book is one that encourages experiments with materials—available materials which stimulate the imagination of teachers, students and others who are creatively active.

Simplicity is stressed to tempt beginners. Professional applications are introduced to show career possibilities.

Materials are reviewed in each chapter because of their importance in suggesting ideas and ways of working.

Ideas for varied activities are offered to guide students of all ages in utilizing their creative energies.

Activities are classified to simplify the organization of materials and eliminate confusion in introducing materials or activities.

In presenting simple procedures to get you started, the author believes that working with materials will lead you to do things in your own way with the materials of your choice. She hopes you will realize that doing things is more important than making things.

One of her aims is to show that one exploration leads to another. Another aim is to record popular ways of working with papier-mâché and new ways created by her friends and herself.

The author hopes that all teachers will realize that, although invention cannot be taught, motivation, perceptive guidance and appreciation are needed to make papier-mâché activities sincere expressions. To create works of art: invention, taste and skill must be combined intelligently as well as emotionally.

ACKNOWLEDGMENTS

So many friends have cooperated wholeheartedly in the preparation of this book that it would be difficult to list each individual who offered suggestions and shared ideas.

I am especially indebted to the following:

Binney and Smith, Inc., for making available illustrations of papier-mâché crafts, designed by their staff of art consultants and artists. Without their encouraging spurs, this book would not have been possible.

School Arts Magazine, for the use of their illustrations of children's work.

Rosemarie Mandarino, for her descriptive pen-and-ink sketches.

Catherine Pilley, for her patience in typing countless drafts of the text.

Charles Betts, my husband, and our daughter, Susan, for their willingness in giving up good times and letting me work quietly in my corner.

V. B. B.

CONTENTS

Crafts, courtesy of Binney & Smith Inc.; photographs
courtesy of McCall's Children's Annual, Volume I.

Chapter One

INTRODUCTION TO PAPIER-MÂCHÉ

Papier-mâché is an excellent inexpensive craft medium inviting wide explorations. Today papier-mâché applies to many types of constructions from the ancient French and Oriental processes used in making pressed paper bowls and trays, to pulp and paper strip modeling, using paper alone or combining paper with other materials.

Creative crafts follow no definite rules since processes vary with individual tastes and discoveries. Exploration, research, varied supplies, discussion and thought will all stimulate creativity.

Creating without preliminary drawings often has many advantages. A direct approach preserves the characteristics of the working materials, eliminates limitations, avoids monotony and a tendency to copy another's design.

Artists, filling an assignment, may prefer to work from their own sketches of planned proportions and required color.

Teachers or parents can use simple demonstrations and discussions to introduce papier-mâché activities to children; but over-direction results in lack of enjoyment since children are rarely concerned with adult ideas of perfection. Their expression is often a simple emotional reaction to a personal experience.

Teachers, students, artists and hobbyists should consider these points when beginning or taking part in a papier-mâché activity:

1. What is the function of the craft?

2. Have you assembled the necessary supplies?

3. Can you construct a solid form; a hollow one?

4. Can you speed or simplify the construction?

5. Will you obtain texture with paper, fabrics, yarns, natural materials, paint?

6. What will you use for hair, eyes, ears, trimmings, trappings?

7. When will you add details—in modeling, in painting, in trimming?

8. How will you paint and protect the completed model?

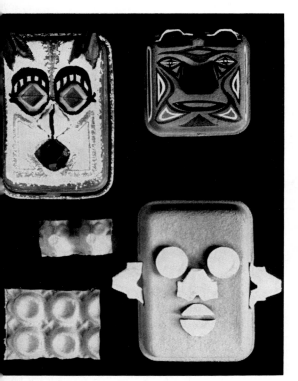

The following chapters provide answers to these questions and many others that will arise during various experiments with papier-mâché.

Papier-mâché crafts have countless practical applications. Some suggestions are:

1. SCHOOLS—Holiday and seasonal projects, puppets and marionettes, animal, bird and human figures, dimensional illustrations and posters, rhythm instruments, gifts, as well as crafts listed for hobby, home, display and theatre.

2. HOBBY—Gifts, containers for dry foods or foliage, trays, costume jewelry, doll-house furniture, toy towns, figurines, lamp bases.

3. HOME—Toys, games, tree ornaments, party favors, home and table decorations, gifts.

12

4. DISPLAY—Mannequins and models, flowers and foliage, dimensional backgrounds, figures.

5. THEATRE AND TELEVISION—Masks, headdresses, stage properties, puppets, marionettes.

Hospitals, recreation centers, camps, churches, play schools and other groups actively interested in the creative crafts can adapt any of these projects to their needs.

An activity plan will stimulate you and be a motivation for improvement and satisfaction. Here are some suggestions:

1. Organize materials and equipment.

2. Let fantasy be your subject matter guide or compile a photographic file of many subjects to study when the real thing is not available.

3. Encourage independent thinking and resourcefulness.

4. Let growth, not perfection, be your concern during your explorations.

5. Develop work habits and originality through creative experiences.

6. Always try an activity before presenting it to others. Show simple examples of basic constructions as well as variety in completed crafts.

13

Photograph, courtesy of Wm. H. Milliken, Jr.

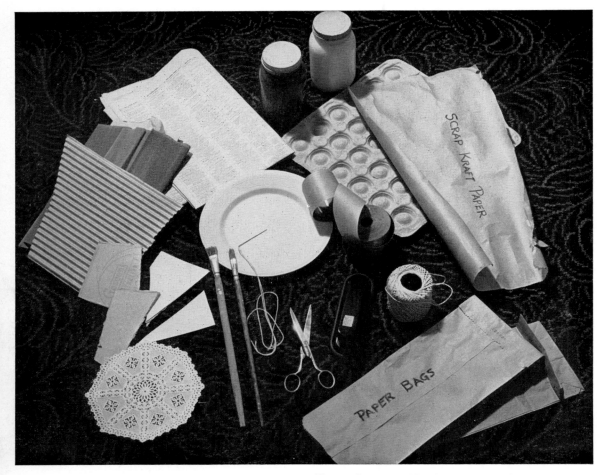

Photograph, courtesy of Bernice Magnie, East Orange, New Jersey.

14

Chapter Two

MATERIALS AND EQUIPMENT

Anyone can create if the proper stimulation is provided. Materials, in themselves, are inspiring and, since experiences in many materials encourage creative growth, a wide selection of adequate materials and required working tools are necessary for motivation and development.

Essential Materials

Essential materials for most papier-mâché crafts are few and inexpensive.

Newspaper.

String and scissors.

Paste and paint.

Optional Materials

Optional materials include many kinds of supplies and offer more opportunities for varied activities.

Papers:

Newspaper, tissue, crepe, unprinted news, brown wrapping, towels, metallic, cardboard, colored construction, corrugated, stencil papers, lace doilies, tape, paper bags, egg and apple carton dividers.

15

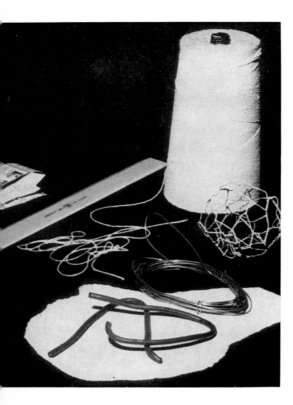

Fasteners:

Rubber bands, string, assorted wire, straight pins, safety pins, stapler.

Adhesives:

Masking tape, gummed tape, adhesive tape, school white paste, wallpaper paste, glue, cement, starch.

Tools:

Rulers, pliers, scissors, brushes, sponges, potatoes and sticks for printing, rubber spatula, saws, hammers, nails, sandpaper, needles, thread.

Strengthening Materials:

Wire, wood, metal, cardboard, plaster of Paris, powdered clay, sawdust, salt, sand, asbestos powder, buckram, cloth strips and scraps.

Cores, Frames, Armatures:

Chicken or turkey wire, baling wire, reed, cartons, crates, tubes, dowels, wood scraps, foil, bowls, fruits, vegetables, gourds, balloons, modeling clay, plastic bottles, umbrella and lampshade frames, styrofoam.

Trimming Materials:

Cotton batting, felt, fabrics, metal foils, flowers, ribbons, feathers, bells, beads,

16

buttons, shells, styrofoam, lace, sequins, watch parts, and other discarded or natural materials.

Art Supplies:

Tempera paint, powder paint, water colors, crayons, modeling clay, finishing varnish, shellac, plastic spray, liquid wax.

Discarded and natural materials are of special value when collected by the student or hobbyist rather than the instructor. Then each will be stimulated by the possibilities of the materials which captured the individual's imagination. Groups should be encouraged to contribute to a general collection.

Uses of Materials

Some suggested uses of inexpensive, natural and discarded materials are helpful for beginners.

Beads, Buttons:

Eyes, costumes, jewelry, headdresses.

Cardboard Cartons:

Cars, houses, miniature furniture, hollow figures, costumes, hats, toys, games, shadow boxes, tunnels, puppets, stages, gifts.

Cloth:

Costumes, for strengthening armatures, stage properties, house furnishings.

17

Dowel Rods:

Supports, cores of figures, marionette controls.

Inner Tubes:

Puppets, toys, games, printing tools.

Mailing Tubes:

Puppets, figures, engines, buildings, trees, lamp bases, ornaments, favors.

Natural Materials:

Cores of figures, stage properties, trimming materials.

Paper Bags:

Hats, masks, costumes, puppets, paper sculpture.

Paper Cups and Plates:

Mobiles, stabiles, hats, costumes, masks, puppets, figures, favors, toys, games.

Wood Scraps:

Dolls, wheels, stick printing, features, favors, supports, buildings, toys, games.

Wire Scraps:

Cores, frames, mobiles, stabiles. supports, trimmings.

18

Equipment

Equipment to improve working conditions is not confined to papier-mâché, but applies to other art activities.

Personal Needs:

Smock, apron or a discarded shirt.

Working Surfaces:

Newspaper or oilcloth to protect furniture, sheets of masonite to provide large table tops.

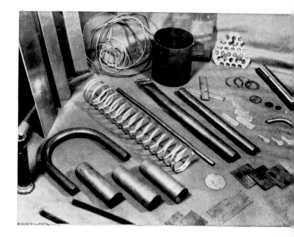

Storage Furniture:

Bookshelves, a discarded cupboard, apple boxes or orange crates.

Storage Containers:

Individual work boxes or market bags for unfinished crafts, shoe boxes, cracker cans, gift cartons, shoe bags, file folders or large strong envelopes, cartons with cardboard partitions for small articles. Label each container.

Art Supply Holders:

Glass jars and plastic containers for paste, paints, water, shellac and brushes—cans or boxes for broken crayons.

Good work habits and responsibility should be developed at home as well as in a club or classroom. Time should be planned for cleaning up and each should do his share. A group can assist in the organization and even in the distribution of materials and equipment. It is wise to have them available and in easily accessible places.

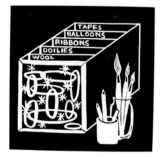

19

Chapter Three

BASIC CONSTRUCTION EXPLORATIONS

It is essential that beginners explore the possibilities of wet and dry papers since all papier-mâché crafts involve one or more ways of working with paper. Newspaper is best for practice work. Later you may wish to work with stronger papers or those that have texture.

Papier-Mâché Pulp

To make enough pulp for several fist-sized models, fill a pail with small pieces of torn paper, cover the paper with water and let it soak overnight. Knead the soaked mass, then squeeze out the excess water by straining the pulp through a sieve or stocking. Add enough paste to hold the mixture together and model the pulp as you would clay. If the pulp tends to crack while drying, press it together and define the modeling on the second day.

Pulp can be mixed with sawdust, salt, sand or asbestos powder. These dry ingredients will require additional paste.

Soft paper napkins or cleansing tissues, generously covered with paste and crumpled, make a softer pulp that is useful for detailed work.

Dry papier-mâché compounds, used by taxidermists and doll hospitals, need water or water and adhesive added to make a strong pulp which can be sanded or carved when dry.

Coils and Twists

To control paper and make it serve your purpose, practice with dry sheets of newspaper which do not tear as easily as wet ones. Strong coils are formed by roll-

21

ing a few sheets toward a folded edge. Insert a layer or two of cloth or a piece of pliable wire for added strength. With string or rubber bands, fasten each coil in the center and at each end.

Twists of paper can be bent into more graceful positions than coils. Roll the paper diagonally for twists, or crush it and give it a slight twist. Insert a piece of wire for strength and flexibility. Wrap the entire length with string to keep the paper from springing apart.

Balls or Wads

Crumple dry paper by pushing the edges of the sheet to the center. Squeeze and shape the wad before adding a string tie. Small sheets of paper with paste spread on one side can be crumpled and used without a tie. Paper bags filled with loosely crumpled papers can be squeezed to change the shape of the wad.

Some constructions can be made of soft wads, while others will need to be built of firm wads. For example, a roast turkey, planned for a stage property, need not be as strong or solid as a doll which will be handled by youngsters.

Pasted Paper Layers

Spread paste generously between layers of dry newspaper to produce a strong thick pad to cut and model while damp. The number of layers is determined by the size and function of the craft. Beginners can try six or eight layers for small shapes, and more for larger ones. Add strength by pasting an occasional layer of cloth between the paper sheets. To save paste, cut a paper pattern of the shape to be modeled by the layer method. Place it on the dry newspaper layers and cut them guided by the pattern. Or with a colored crayon, draw the outlines of the required shapes on the top sheet of newspaper before the papers have been pasted together. After pasting the sheets together, cut out the shapes within the crayon outline so the crayon marks will not interfere with the painted surface decoration.

Pasted paper layers must be bent and shaped while damp, so allow time to model them. Do not spread the paste until you have planned your pattern.

Sculptured Papers

Fold, cut, curl or tear various dry papers for sculptured trimmings. Strengthen thin novelty papers with pasted backings of cloth or paper. Include hinge-flaps when cutting paper features or costume parts to aid in fastening the additions.

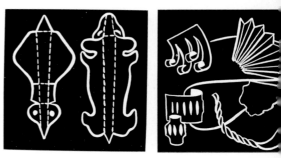

Photographs, courtesy of Hilda Rath, Park Ridge, New Jersey.

Working with Newspaper Strips

Tear paper from the fold down or along a ruler's edge. The width of the strip is determined by the area to be covered. Whip school white paste to a creamy consistency for easy spreading and greater coverage. For fast drying, cover only one side of a dry strip with paste. For slower drying, pull the strips through a dish of paste. Strips can also be applied between coats of paste. Strips dipped in liquid starch will add stiffness between the pasted paper layers. Torn paper pieces can be used instead of strips.

Working with Novelty Papers

Cut any papers which do not tear easily. Heavy papers often require more paste and more time to stretch. Corrugated and metallic papers

may need cement or glue instead of paste. Papers which tend to spring and curl can be tied in place with rag strips during the drying process. Tissue and other thin papers are easier to handle when not too moist. Crepe paper strips can be used dry for a taut binding. A textured paper provides an unusual surface when used for the last layer.

Working with Paste

Be generous with paste to obtain a smooth top surface. Cover one entire side of the paper to let it stretch evenly. While applying a paste-covered strip, pull the paper gently and rub the surface to eliminate wrinkles or air pockets. Count the number of layers or observe the distribution of paste and paper by alternating printed newsprint with colored comics or with paper towels.

School white paste will spread easily and go further if it is beaten before use. Fingers, a stiff brush or a spatula will spread the paste. Keep a damp cloth handy for wiping sticky hands.

Photograph, courtesy of Cooper Union, New York City.

Padding

Cores of paper, wood, wire or other materials can be built up with dry or damp crumpled wads; with sections of pasted

25

layers, or with cloth or cotton batting which has been fastened with string or tape to the core. A smooth firm surface is obtained by adding a few layers of well-pasted strips.

Working with Objects to be Removed

When working over clay models, dishes, fruits, vegetables, bottles, rubber balls and other objects, use a layer or two of wet paper to cover the form and keep the pasted paper from sticking to it. Then add pasted pieces or strips, using a different kind of paper for alternate layers. Six to ten layers are usually enough for small forms; more layers are needed for larger and stronger ones. When the pasted paper is dry, lift off the shell. Split a shell that completely covers an object and fasten the halves together with more paste-covered strips.

Any area of the shell that was next to the core object can be finished by adding a layer of pasted paper. Rough edges of paper shells (bowls, masks, etc.) can be finished with overlapping pasted strips.

Working with Breakable Objects

When covering glass, brittle plastic, balloons or thin-shelled gourds, use enough layers of pasted paper to make a strong shell.

Papier-Mâché Casts in Plaster Molds

Papier-mâché masks, puppet heads, and other crafts can be made with paper pulp or pasted strips which are pressed into a plaster mold. Vaseline, baby oil, or two layers of wet paper will keep the paste from sticking to the plaster. Pulp halves can be cemented together while halves of paper shells can be fastened with pasted paper strips.

Let these guides be beginning experiences. Have you tried cores of bunched cloth or fistfuls of excelsior? Is gummed paper available—for strong speedy bindings? Continue to explore the possibilities offered by many other materials.

27

Photographs of puppets appearing above and on pages 29, 30 and 31, made in classes at Teachers'
College, Columbia University; courtesy of Bernice Magnie, Art Supervisor, East Orange, New Jersey.

Chapter Four

PAPER BAG CREATURES

Essential Equipment

Paper: Bags, newspaper, colored and metallic papers, cardboard, corrugated paper, mailing tubes.

Fasteners: Safety pins, brass paper fasteners, a stapler, tapestry needles and strong thread, gummed tape, string, school white paste.

Tools and Paint: Scissors, tempera or powder paint, brushes, crayons.

Constructions

Toy-like dolls, hand or rod puppets and string puppets, all made of paper bags, appeal to children for games and plays. Even tiny tots can make simple ones while advanced students are challenged by more intricate constructions.

1. Paper bag creatures are fast and easy to make, and encourage beginners. Stuff crumpled or shredded newspaper into a bag bottom and tie a string to indicate the neck. The rest of the bag is painted to indicate a costume. Arms and legs may be flat cut papers or cardboards stapled, taped or sewn to the bag.

2. A variation is to start with a long bag. Crush and stuff newspaper for the head, tie at the neck, add more crushed papers and tie again. Use the rest of the bag as a tail or add more stuffing for a full skirt. The bag bottom can also be split and stuffed for trousers. Any open or cut seams are stapled together. Try flat paper, rolls of paper, twists or folds for arms, legs, horns, ears or beaks.

3. Still another plan is to use separate bags for heads and bodies. Experiment with the head bag to see if parts can be shaped for hat, hair, ears or a collar. Use staples, or paste and paper strips as fasteners.

4. In making both human and animal figures, stuff the bags and turn them in all directions for ideas. Try folding and squeezing

sections to help the shape develop and feel free to add more bags to make your figure grow. Reach for paper rolls, cones or twists, when they are needed.

5. Animal heads with protruding jaws require more thought and effort. Use less stuffing for the jaws and tie or tape that end of the bag to form the nose and mouth. Or use two bags of different sizes, stapled together where the bridge of the nose meets the forehead. Bend, fold, slash and staple the large "forehead bag" to suggest a neck. Experiment with the jaws. Can you make them open and close? Would you like to insert teeth or a tongue?

Action

Think about the purpose of the bag creature. How flexible shall it be? Do you want to make the toy move by adding strings? In what other ways can action be provided?

Not all paper bag toys are strung as marionettes. They can be hand or rod puppets, masks or parts of a mechanical display.

Figure action is improved by fastening arms and legs so they will dangle.

30

Bouncing legs and arms can be made of a "cat stairs fold." Staple or paste two strips of cut paper at right angles. Fold the strips back and forth over each other. Fasten ends to the body and to cutouts of hands and feet. It is easier to add color and designs to large sheets of paper before cutting the long narrow strips.

Keep the stuffing soft and pliable for flexibility. Staple the arms, legs and body at the "bending joints" for more action. Make a "hinge joint," which moves in only two directions (back and forth), by stapling one flat edge to another. Try a "rotary hinge" by loosely sewing one part to another. Leave some space between the parts for free action in all directions.

Twist papers and tie them at each end or sometimes wrap the entire length of the twist with string to give it strength. Use these for pliable appendages. Even paper braids and chains make amusing arms and legs.

Stringing before painting simplifies drying and storage problems. Beginners often use only one string with each end fastened to an arm. Another string can have an end attached to each leg—or to a head and tail.

Painting and Trimming

Cut, torn and curled papers (for noses, ears, hair, etc.) can be added with paste or staples before paint is used, or sculptured, colored or decorated papers can be added after the paint has dried.

Painting is an exciting adventure, for suddenly a drab figure can come to life and take on a colorful appearance as well as a colorful personality.

Paper cups and plates, lace doilies, ribbons, wool, feathers or flowers—will tempt you to add fanciful costume accessories.

Exaggeration of essential characteristics, both in construction and in painting, will de-

31

velop a puppet personality. Exaggerate position and color to portray a mood. Carry the mood into the scenery.

A simple stage for a paper bag marionette show is the floor, with a table, turned on its side, for the background. Stand behind the table while working the string controls. Tape large paintings to the table top for scenery. Think about the story and the action while making the paper bag creature, while painting and trimming it and while practicing the action. A completely original show will delight the audience and provide surprises for all.

Photograph, courtesy of David E. Crespi, Southern Connecticut State College, New Haven, Connecticut.

Chapter Five

SOLID PAPER PEOPLE

Essential Equipment

Paper:	Newspaper, paper towels, paper bags, cardboard.
Cores:	Wire, tubes, boxes, socks, cloth bags, strong cord.
Fasteners:	String, rubber bands, adhesive tape, socks, paste.
Tools and Paint:	Scissors, mat knife, tempera or powder paint, brushes.

Experimental Approach

Make an assortment of balls, wads, coils and twists of various sizes. Arrange them in different combinations and positions to whet and develop your imagination. Make a long, fat, loose roll of newspaper. Squeeze and tie it at the neck and waist to suggest a simple chubby figure. Fasten another loose roll at the shoulder level for arms. Bend the paper at the waist for action. Can you make the paper hold its shape? Have you tied it firmly? Do you need wire? Perhaps mailing tubes, paper cups or boxes, stuffed with paper, will offer fresh impetus for your imagination.

Pulp Experiments

Combine pulp with other ingredients. Model pulp over firm paper wads or over coils strengthened with pasted strips. Stuff a sock or a cloth bag with pulp. Model and tie the figure with the pulp in the bag or sock. When the pulp is dry, paint the cloth, or cut it away before painting the pulp.

33

Coils, twists and wads of newspaper can be used to construct cores for solid figures. Wire cores are useful for slender figures.

Pre-planned Approach

Creative work can be stimulated by a presentation of assorted paper shapes—coils, wads, twists, cones, cylinders, a square or rectangular form.

These steps will simplify the process: Think. Decide on the size, shape and position of the figure. Make the required paper or wire coils, or twists and wads of paper. Fasten them together firmly with string or tape. Develop the contour of the figure with added wads of dry paper, tied or pasted. Add any desired paper features. Paste a few layers of dry, torn newspaper strips over the entire figure. When dry, paint the figure with tempera or powder paint.

Simple Figures for Beginners

1. Make two long coils or twists. Fasten each separate end. Hold the coils or twists, side by side and tie the centers together. Bend the top third of the double roll forward, squeeze and tie at the neck. The four extensions become arms and legs.

2. Use the above plan, but, after bending the coils forward, add a head of crumpled paper. A square of paper, wrapped over the head wad and squeezed and tied at the neck, will have loose ends to attach to the shoulders.

3. Shape and tie two crumpled wads for a head and a body. Bend two long coils into narrow arches to straddle the shoulders of the body wad. Add a tight belt of string. Slip a third long coil under the top of the arches to build up the shoulders and supply arms. Tie the head wad on top of the body wad.

34

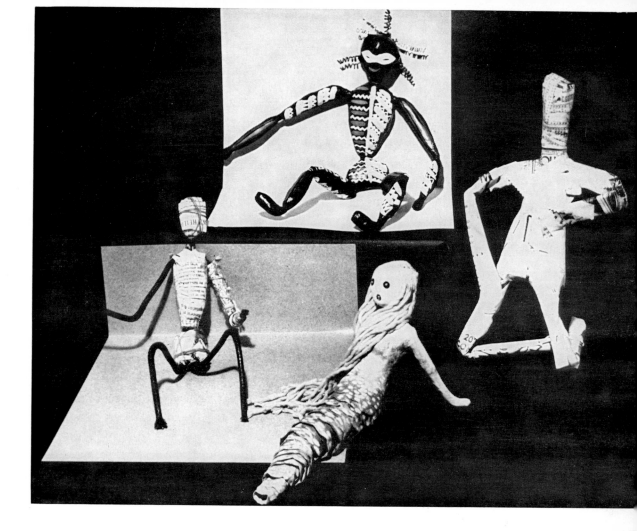

Action Figures

Figures that bend when dry can be designed with a different plan. Make of scrap telephone wire, or other strong, flexible wires, a thin figure core which is similar to a simple line drawing. Use a continuous length, or as few wire pieces as absolutely necessary. Double the wire, if you need strength. Mark the wire to indicate the joints where the figure bends. Indicate neck, shoulder, elbow, wrist, waist, hip, knee, ankle. (Very large projects can include the joints in hands and feet.) With dry wads, pad the parts of the figure between the marked joints. Be sure to leave the wire exposed at all joints. Paste dry newspaper

35

or paper towel strips over the wadded sections. If you wish, reinforce the exposed wire joints with a few layers of narrow adhesive tape.

Action figures are helpful to determine positions for sketches. They can be dolls or mannequins for dress designing and are excellent teaching aids for sports and other activities.

Paper Bead Figures

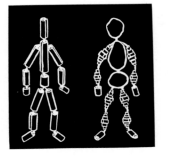

Sections of legs and arms for flexible action dolls or marionettes can be made of paper beads strung on a core figure of leather strips or strong cord. Some beads are made by spreading paste on one side of a long dry strip of drawing paper and winding the strip on a lollipop stick. Or, beads of pulp can be modeled on the stick. Use pulp or dry paper wads covered with paste and newspaper for variety in making heads and bodies.

Sandwich Shapes

Papier-mâché figures which appear stiff and resemble slabs involve another construction method. On cardboard which can be cut easily with shears or a mat knife, draw an outline or silhouette of the figure. Cut it out and make a duplicate. Use the two cutouts as you would two slices of bread and add a firm filling of paper wads. Moisten the cardboard edges, if you wish to bend or round them. Wrap the "filled sandwich" with string and wind pasted paper strips around it. You can build out the flat sides, or extend the filling with more crumpled wads of paper and pasted strips which hold the wads in place. Combine the sandwich plan with paper-stuffed boxes and other construction methods.

36

Chapter Six

SOLID BIRDS AND ANIMALS

Essential Equipment

Paper:	Newspaper, paper bags.
Cores:	Wire, dowels, sticks, tubes.
Fasteners:	String, rubber bands, paste.
Trimmings:	Colored paper, feathers, etc.
Tools and Paint:	Scissors, tempera or powder paint, crayons.

Exploration

Combine paper wads and coils in various ways. Can you tie or tape them together to hold a position? Is it easier for you to stuff a paper bag with crumpled paper and squeeze it into shape? Will you need braces of wire or sticks? It is fun to enter a world of fantasy and bring forth a two-headed tiger or six-legged stork!

Paper pulp used alone or mixed with other materials can be used as a self-hardening clay or applied in a thick layer on a firm dry paper bird or animal.

Planning

Decide on the size, shape and position of the bird or animal and follow the suggestions in Chapter 5 to complete the craft.

Simple Animals

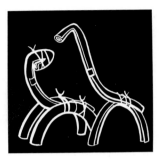

1. Make two long and wide coils of paper. Fasten all ends with string or rubber bands. Bend one roll into an arch. Put the second coil on top of the arch to make a thicker body, a neck, a head and a tail. Fasten the coils together at the top of the arch. Bend the neck, head and tail into position. Add string and pasted paper strips. Paint division lines in the legs.

2. Vary the above plan by starting with *three* coils; bend two into leg arches and slip the third coil between the two and fasten firmly at the top of the arch. The third coil will broaden the body and also provide a neck and head. Pad the head and body and reinforce all parts with pasted strips.

3. Strong, fat animals can be assembled with two very long coils and two or three crumpled wads. Place the ends of the two coils under the head wad and tie them to it. Then tie the coils to a neck wad (if neck padding is needed) and continue with the coils under the body wad. Go down and up with the coils for strong double coil front legs, add a string belt at the stomach and continue down and up for back legs. Continue the coils around the back and tie string, lengthwise, around the body to keep the coils in place.

4. Using three long coils of paper or wire or three paper twists (the length and thickness depend on the design), bend two coils into arches for legs and use the third for the body, neck and head. Let the leg arches straddle the body or tie them under the body. Try figure 8

40

loops of string to connect each front leg to a rear leg and to connect front legs and rear legs. These loops will keep the legs from springing apart. Now you can pad your pet (or wild animal) and cover it with pasted paper strips.

5. Use the three coils for another core, but this time make wider leg arches. Place each arch lengthwise under the body and tie it to the body coil. Each arch will provide one front and one rear leg. Pad, cover with pasted paper, dry, paint, decorate. Bend 1 or 2 wire hangers for the core, pad the animal with crumpled paper. Fasten the padding with string and pasted strips.

Separate heads, built up on a dowel, can be stuck into an animal or bird body and can be turned expressively. When making the body, build the wads over an extending hollow cardboard tube so the dowel has a place to fit.

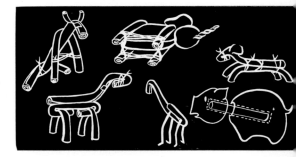

Action Birds and Animals

Birds and animals that bend when dry can be constructed of pasted paper wads and strips pasted on a core of flexible wire. Leave the wire exposed at the joints to permit action. Wrap the wire joints with a few layers of pasted cloth to thicken them.

41

Sandwich Silhouettes

On lightweight cardboard, draw two identical profile outlines of a bird or animal. Cut out the silhouettes and insert a filling of crumpled paper between the two cardboards. Dampen the cardboards with a wet cloth, if you decide to round the edges. Wrap the "sandwich silhouette" with a few layers of pasted newspaper strips.

If the stiff stylized creature does not please you, add crumpled wads to give roundness.

Simple Birds

1. Stuff one corner of a long paper bag with crumpled papers, squeeze and tie it at the neck. Do you see a beak? Insert more crumpled paper and tie again. Does the unfilled open end of the bag suggest a tail? Can you split it and fold the ends forward for wings? Can you fasten legs of strong wire or sticks to the body?

2. Make a long loose twist of paper. Fold an end over, squeeze and tie it for a head. Wind part of the twist with string to indicate a neck. Roll the other end over and over for the body and fasten. Cover the bird with pasted paper strips.

3. Crumple two wads and tie one to another for a head and a body.

4. Crumple a wad for a body. Take a large sheet of newspaper; place the wad in the center; gather the loose corners and twist them for a neck and head. Fold over the end of the twist to enlarge the head.

Suggestions

Legs can be paper or wire coils bent into an arch and tied to the body. Or sticks or twigs can be stuck into the body for legs. Since feathers are graceful and fragile, perhaps you would like to add wings and tail of paper sculpture. The cut papers can be folded, coiled or curled. Sometimes, real feathers supply decorative accents. Try stiff fabrics or layers of pasted newspaper cut into wing and tail shapes.

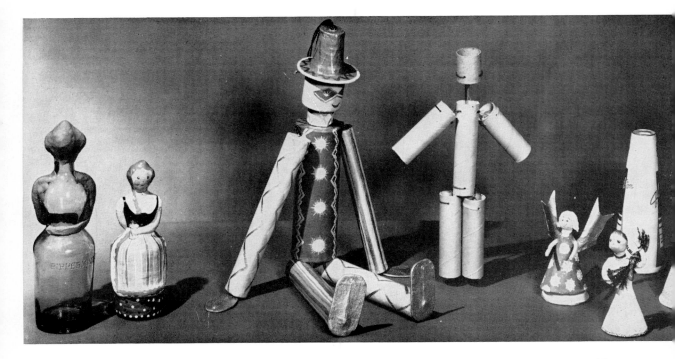

Chapter Seven

HOLLOW PAPER PEOPLE

Essential Materials and Equipment

Newspaper	Boxes	Plastic Bottles
Paste	Tubes	Sticks
Scissors	Fruits	Wire
String	Vegetables	Small Stones
Tape	Gourds	Paper Towels
Stapler	Bottles	Tissue Paper
Paints	Cans	Aluminum Foil
Crayons	Balloons	Poultry Wire
Nonhardening Clay	Light Bulbs	Wood Scraps
Picnic Spoons	Paper Cups	Trimmings

Experimental Approach

Collect different kinds of discarded boxes, light bulbs, hollow balls, gourds, bottles, cans, balloons and other hollow objects in assorted sizes. Try many combinations of the hollow objects to see which suggest human figures in various positions. Select the shapes you prefer, fasten them together with string, wire, staples or strong gummed tape. Add layers of pasted strips for strength and to provide an absorbent surface for paint. While pasting, feel free to add contour with wads, or braces with coils.

Planned Approach

When you have decided upon the size, shape and function of your model, obtain the hollow objects, as well as the other materials needed for the process. If you cannot find hollow discarded or inexpensive cartons to fill your need, consider other methods of hollow construction described and applied in this chapter for figures, and the methods suggested in Chapter 8 for hollow birds and animals.

Some Simple Folks

1. Try a paper- and paste-covered light bulb head stuck in a cardboard tube. Pad the base of the bulb with crumpled paper for a firm fit and fasten it to the tube with pasted strips of newspaper. Speed your craft with arms of cut paper, fabric or yarn.

2. Vary this plan by crushing the tops of two paper towel tubes around the base of the paper-covered bulb and securing them. Add arms of paper coils or twists. Pad the body, if you wish. Dress the figure with paper, cloth or paint.

3. Use a paper-covered ball, a light bulb or a gourd to provide a head in the top of a box body. Model features with soft tissue and paste. Cut out armholes and insert a long coil or twist for arms. Cut out leg holes to insert paper tube legs. Or make slits at the tops of the tubes, bend the flaps out and paste them under the box body. Wrap clay or small stones in paper for feet. Stuff the twisted corners of the paper into the bottoms of the tube legs. Secure the feet in position with pasted strips.

4. Try space sculpture figures. Perhaps some cartoon creatures can be inspired by the phrases: "hollow leg," "empty-headed," "a frog in his throat." Cut windows in front and back of the carton or tube. Bind the frame edges with pasted strips. If needed, make tiny models of clay or paper to fit the space and complete the description. Toy miniatures can also be combined with the space sculptures.

46

Chicken Wire Modeling

Chicken or turkey wire is flexible and can be shaped for both curved and angular forms. For a large project or a top-heavy small one, start with a core and a base of wood or metal. Break or bend, saw and nail the core in the desired position. Cut measured pieces of wire mesh to model for each separate armature section. Slip the modeled sections over the core and attach them to each other by entwining the mesh edges. Use additional flexible wire strands to fasten the model to the base.

When the frame is shaped and secured to the base, it is ready for paste and paper and later when dry, for paint and shellac.

Chicken and turkey wire, and even window screening are practical materials for large projects. Combine wire mesh with large cartons for stage properties, parade pieces or displays. Include wire-cutting pliers and heavy gloves in your equipment.

Clay and Carton Modeling

Often, a carton, cone or bottle will whet your imagination, but is incomplete in itself. On these shapes, provide identity by adding nonhardening, oil-based clay for contour or features. Cover the clay area with thin aluminum foil to keep the oil from seeping through the paper coats. Add layers of pasted paper over the entire craft. If you wish to re-use the clay and carton model, start with a layer of wet paper before adding pasted paper layers. Cut the dry shell in two, remove the core and fasten the shell together with pasted strips.

Photograph, courtesy of Wm. H. Milliken, Jr.

47

Chapter Eight

HOLLOW BIRDS AND ANIMALS

Essential Materials and Equipment

Newspaper	Hollow Cartons	Balloons
Paste	Tubes	Sticks
String	Fruits	Wires
Tape	Vegetables	Modeling Clay
Stapler	Gourds	Paints
Scissors	Bottles	Trimmings

Exploration

Use hollow objects singly or combine them to suggest various poses of birds and animals. Change the objects when the shape does not please you and try different combinations. Join the selected parts with string or tape and then reinforce the creation with several layers of paste and paper. Let hollow objects suggest realistic or abstract birds and animals or lead you into a world of make-believe as you create members of a never-ever zoo.

Planning

When your scrap collection does not contain the needed hollow objects, hunt further for cartons of special sizes or extra strength. You may want large boxes to wear, to ride, or to use in parades or display. Strong cord, heavy gummed paper and wire will fasten large objects together and make a sturdy object.

49

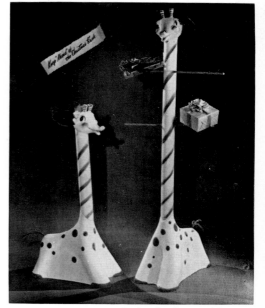

Designed and executed by
Richard Rush Studios, Chicago, Illinois

Both small and large objects can be built up with paper wads and coils for contour or for braces. String, tape and pasted layers will secure them in position.

Carton Creatures

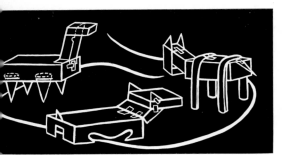

Select your containers and plan the arrangement. Make cutout holes or slits in the body carton for inserts of head, neck, legs or tail parts. Staple them in place, or use gummed tape instead. Pasted paper layers will strengthen any creature and will provide an absorbent painting surface when waxed containers are used for the base of one.

Comical, Conical Creatures

Make long and short, thin and fat cones of newspaper layers or of pliable cardboard. Use cellophane or masking tape to hold the cone shape. Or wrap the cone with a sheet of paper which has paste spread over one side. Cut holes or slits to fit one cone to another and secure them with pasted strips. Combine cartons and cones for variety. Use paper cup cones or conical cartons, if you wish.

Gourds

Gourds are often graceful and expressive. The twist or turn of a narrowing top may suggest dignity, sorrow or curiosity. Do you remember the popular "Schmoo" which first appeared in gourd country? Create your own fantasy from a gourd base. Combine gourds with cartons or cones and cover the entire shape with layers of pasted strips.

Bases for Papier-Mâché Shells

Model clay forms or use fruits and vegetables as a base. These forms used alone or combined with each other or with bottles, gourds or other preformed shapes, will be helpful. A bit of clay can be used in fastening several objects together or they can be tied or taped. Remember that a layer of wet paper is needed to keep the pasted paper layers from sticking, if the core is to be removed for re-use. Cover the creature with layers of pasted strips. Leave the hollow objects in the paper shell or cut the shell apart and fasten sections together with more paste and paper.

Chicken Wire Constructions

Chicken and turkey wire, window wire or plastic screening can be cut, bent and fastened to form large birds or animals. Chapter 7 contains directions for modeling procedures.

Balloon Modeling

Blow up odd-shaped balloons to use as a base for layers of paste and paper. Or create more unusual shapes by squeezing and taping partially inflated round balloons. Achieve a still wider variety of form by taping several balloons together. Securely fasten all balloons to retain the air. Cover them with six or more layers of dry newspaper pieces and paste. Strips of thin cloth, wet with liquid starch, will provide added stiffness when inserted between the pasted paper layers.

Make appealing rhythm toys or noisy birds and animals by dropping some rice grains or dried peas in the balloons before they are inflated. These and other balloon-based inventions, gayly painted, are effective when suspended.

Chapter Nine

GUIDES FOR HAND PUPPETS

Essential Materials

Paper: Newspaper, small bags, towels, flexible cardboard.

Fasteners: Paste, rubber bands, needle and thread, safety pins.

Cores: Cardboard tubes, dowels, nonhardening clay, balloons, socks and gloves, wire.

Tools and Trimmings: Scissors, mat knife, fabrics, yarn, tempera or powder paints, water colors, crayons.

Puppetry is an enjoyable activity from the making of the puppet to the performance of the play. Hand puppets are usually manipulated by the index finger which is inserted in the head, and the thumb and middle finger, extended to work the arm and hand action. Collect or make hollow coils of strong paper or flexible cardboard to fit the three fingers. With the tubes on the fingers, practice the action.

Explore the many ways of modeling heads and constructing hands. Allow part of the tubes to extend as neck and wrists so costumes can be attached. Consider modeling shoulders of paper, at the base of the neck tube, to provide a support for the costumes.

Some Ways of Modeling Heads

1. Crumple and squeeze dry newspaper over the top of a hollow tube which fits over the index finger. Hold it in place with string or a rubber band. Cover one side of a 12- or 15-inch square of newspaper, or a paper towel, with paste. Place the top of the head in the center of the square and draw the four corners down to cover the head and neck. Wrinkle part of the cover to model features. Crumple the corners to form small shoulders.

2. Stuff a sock foot with paper pulp. Insert a dowel, which is a bit larger than the index finger. Model the head, neck and shoulders too, if you wish. Use string or pasted strips of dry paper to keep the head from sagging. When dry, remove the dowel.

3. Model on a wooden dowel, a head and neck of papier-mâché pulp or asbestos powder mixed with paste and water. If the pulp tends to sag, let the head dry overnight and redefine the features on the following day.

4. Stuff a small paper bag with dry crumpled paper. Insert a tube and add a tie around the bag and tube at the neck. Features can be painted on the bag or they can be modeled of soft damp paper, held in place with dry pasted strips.

5. Crumple and stuff paste-covered paper in a paper cup. Model or drape some of the paper for hair or features. Poke a hole in the bottom of the cup for index finger action. Let "cuppets" suggest the use of small boxes and paper cones for puppet heads.

6. Let a fairly large tube be the head and neck of the puppet. Add features of pulp, wads

and pasted strips, or of sculptured papers. The top of the tube can be part of a hat.

7. Start with a large doubled sheet of dry newspaper. Fold over a diagonal corner about half the size of a lady's handkerchief. Pick up the sheet and wind the folded corner around the index finger to form the neck. Hold the neck roll in place with the thumb of the same hand. Crumple the sheet loosely as you roll the rest of the cone forward to make a head. Put a rubber band around the head. Develop the features with pasted wads and strips. Pasted pieces of paper will keep the modeled, dry, crumpled paper in position.

8. Crumple two egg-sized wads of dry paper. Place one on each side of the top of a hollow tube. Squeeze them while adding a string tie. Add features of pulp or of paper wads and pasted strips.

9. Insert the neck of a deflated balloon through a paper tube a bit larger than the index finger. Blow up the balloon to puppet head size and tie it tightly to keep the air from escaping. Cover the head and the neck tube with six or more layers of paste-covered strips. Model features of tissue which has been covered with paste and crumpled.

10. Model a simple head, neck and shoulders of nonhardening oil-based clay. Cover the clay with one layer of wet paper, then six or eight layers of dry pasted strips or pieces. When dry, dig out the clay or cut the paper shell apart, remove the clay, and fasten the halves together with pasted strips. If clay is not available, use a darning egg or an electric light bulb as the core.

55

Suggestions for Constructing Puppet Hands

1. Let your own finger tips extend beyond the puppet sleeves.

2. Use narrow tubes, cut and painted or coils of oaktag, squeezed and tied.

3. Cut and shape gummed brown paper.

4. Model pulp hands on each end of a dowel. Slip off when dry.

5. Use ends of glove fingers, or cut and sewn hands of flannel, felt or chamois, sewn on the costume sleeves.

6. Tie ends of puppet sleeves, cut and sewn into hand shapes. Wide sleeves can be gathered at the wrist.

7. Apply one layer of wet paper and about six layers of paste and paper over clay models of hands. Dig out the clay when the paper shell feels dry.

8. Use doll wardrobe accessories or miniature novelties (boxing gloves, knitted mittens, etc.).

9. Make cloth miniature mittens, sewn to indicate fingers. If puppet hands are large, stuff each finger.

10. Bend covered wire or pipe cleaners into finger and hand shapes. Strengthen the wire frame with tape or pasted paper strips. Pad and cover with sewn gloves of soft cloth.

Suggestions for Costumes

Puppet clothes must be roomy enough for hand action and costumes must be designed with

56

the action in mind. Consider the size and strength of the live actor's hand in planning both puppet and costume. When time is limited, make the costumes simple and aim for effective impressions of the authentic designs. Beginners can experiment with soft paper for patterns.

1. Use a large circle of cloth with cutout neck and armholes.

2. Fold over the top half of a vertical rectangle (twice as long as its width). With the crease at the top, fold the doubled sheet into a booklet. Draw and cut out ¼ of a circle at the upper folded corner to make the neck opening. Draw and cut the under sleeve line at the other side. Open the booklet and split the neck opening in back so the gown can slip over the head. Open the cloth, lay it on a smooth flat surface, crayon a costume, press the wax crayon to set the color, sew the seams and hem, bind the neck opening and attach any desired trimmings.

3. Measure a horizontal rectangle with a top hem wide enough for a drawstring neckline. Cut out armholes beneath the neckline hem. Measure and mark ¼ and ¾ of the distance from one rectangle side for the armholes. To include a gathered collar in the pattern, sew both edges of a soft tape or ribbon to the back of the costume an inch or two below the top hem. Leave openings at each end for a drawstring.

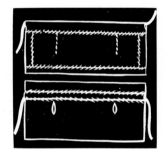

4. Design a simple foundation gown of unbleached muslin as a base for elaborate costumes. Stuffed legs can be sewn to the front of the gown.

Puppets can change character with costume changes. Aid the change by sewing wigs to costume hats. Puppet hair can be modeled of paper or made of hair, wool, wire, cord, steel wool, cotton or fabric pasted or cemented to the head.

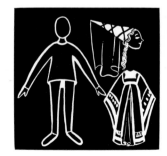

Costume impressions can be obtained quickly and easily with crayon or paint applied to simple muslin gowns. Shellac will protect the colors and give body to the fabric when it is needed.

57

Chapter Ten

GUIDES FOR MARIONETTES

Essential Equipment

Newspaper	Cloth Tape	Metal Rings
Paste	Fabrics	Weights
String	Dowels	Wire
Scissors	Scrap Wood	Crayons
Stapler	Screw Eyes	Water Colors
Needles	Screens	Tempera Paint
Thread	Screw Driver	Brushes
Straight Pins	Hammer	Shellac
Safety Pins	Tacks	Trimmings

Essential Materials

String-controlled puppets are called marionettes. They require more time and patience than hand puppets. In creating a doll that moves, observation of figure proportions and body action are primary needs. There should also be an awareness of thickness, as well as of height and width, since the figures may be seen from all angles.

Simple and speedy marionettes, made of stuffed paper bags, were discussed in Chapter 3. Stronger and more varied models can be made of papier-mâché pulp or pasted wads and strips on a flexible core. Regardless of the materials used, all marionettes should be planned so that the joints move freely.

Marionette making is an art that has been popular for centuries. Start with these simple constructions and explore a new and fascinating hobby.

Hollow Marionette Heads

Often hollow hand puppet heads, described in Chapter 9, can be adapted to marionette use by adding or including loops from which to attach the control strings.

1. Form a cross of strong cloth tape and knot the tapes where they cross. Sew tiny metal rings to each of the four tape ends. Let the rings extend when joining the split shell of a papier-mâché puppet head.

2. Make a cross of twisted wire with loops at each end and insert it in the same way as the tape cross. Stuff the head and neck with crumpled paper to keep the neck loop in position.

3. Use ⅜″ dowels for the cross. Whittle shallow notches so the dowels will fit where they cross. Add tape or wire to strengthen the cross formation. Insert the cross in the split puppet head. Let a screw eye at each end extend beyond the paper shell. Join the two halves of the puppet head together with pasted strips of paper.

If the hollow puppet heads are not split, control loops can be added in other ways.

4. Use gummed cloth tape to fasten bent hairpins or long V-shaped wires to the outside of the head. Cover the cloth tape with paste and paper. Pierce holes near the base of the neck so a cloth body can be sewn to the neck.

5. Sew tiny metal rings (or use tiny safety pins), at each end of a narrow ribbon tape. Place the center of the tape under the chin and bring the ends up so the rings extend above and behind the ears. Fasten the tape in place with pasted paper strips. Another tape strip, with a ring at the center, can be placed across the neck opening and the ends stapled to the sides of the neck. The ring should hang below the base of the neck.

Solid Marionette Heads

Solid heads can be modeled of paper pulp, of dry crumpled paper with top layers of pasted strips, or of paper mixtures (paper and paste mixed with sawdust, salt, wax, asbestos, or other materials).

Control loops can be inserted and cemented in any solid head.

Paper modeling can be done over any of these cores: discarded light bulbs, gourds, nest eggs, dowels, balls.

Simplify and exaggerate the features for an effective puppet character. Pencils, brush handles, paper clips, orange sticks and spoons are helpful modeling tools when pulp is used.

61

Simple Marionette Figures

Bodies for human or animal marionettes can be made of dowels, of wood scraps, of cardboard tubes and cartons, of shaped chicken wire, of pulp and other paper compounds, and of cloth. Observation of proportion and of action is required since the figure must be designed for free movement.

1. SOLID PAPIER-MÂCHÉ BODIES—An armature of ½″ to 1″ wide strips of strong tape, or leather, or rubber inner tubes, can be marked to indicate the joints. Sections of the body between action joints are then padded with paste and paper as shown in Chapter 5. Weight hands and feet with lead pellets fastened to the armature with pasted paper.

Another simple figure is made by knotting at one end, four rag strips or four discarded stockings. The knot can be the head core, two strips are used as cores for arms and two for legs. Shorten the arm strips if you are designing a human figure instead of an animal. Make bands of folded paper to outline the body sections and thread the strips through holes cut in the bands. Leave the cloth exposed at all joints for free action when the head knot, the body sections, the arms and the legs are padded with wads and pasted strips.

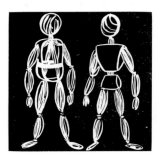

2. HOLLOW PAPER FIGURES—Make slender cones of strong paper for arm and leg sections, hands and feet. Bend in half, long rectangles of paper for head, chest and hip sections. Overlap the corners of the open ends to narrow the chin and waist. Fasten each cone and folded rectangle with staples or paste to hold the shape. Slip a long cloth tape through the top of the shoulder section and thread the arm and hand cones on each end. Slip another cloth tape through the bottom of the hip section and thread the leg and foot cones on each end. Make a slit the width of the tape in the top center fold of the head, the top center fold of the chest and the bottom center fold of the hip. Insert a tape through the body and staple it to the paper at each slit. Leave ½″ of the tape exposed for neck and waist action.

62

When stapling the cones to the tape, allow enough exposed tape to permit free joint action.

Instead of threading the hollow cone sections, try making free action joints of cotton batting and wrap them and the adjoining paper areas with pieces of paste-covered fabric.

3. WOODEN BODIES—Select the needed wooden pieces and attach them to each other with small screw eyes. Use a thumbtack to make the small opening for the screw eye. Pad the head and neck dowel with modeled paper. Thin wooden bodies also can be padded with paper.

4. CLOTH-STUFFED BODIES—Make an original paper pattern; cut and stitch a cloth body. Leave the top seams open. Stuff the body with crumpled paper, rags, kapok, sawdust or a mixture of materials. Include sawdust or lead pellets where weights are needed. Use very loose stuffing and a few rows of stitching at the joints to permit free action.

(a) Stuff and sew the shoulder seams, then sew the neck to the base of a hollow puppet.
(b) Or insert a shoulder dowel (with screw eyes at each end and in the top center), stuff and sew, letting the rings extend.
(c) Include a cloth head and neck in designing your paper marionette pattern. Make papier-mâché masks, attached to tight-fitting skull caps—to change your puppet character. Hair and hats can also be attached to the skull cap.

SUGGESTIONS—Have you tried discarded shoulder pads for marionettes? Combine various materials in constructing action figures. Explore ways of providing action joints when novel materials like straw, plastic lacing, etc., are used. Feel free to create new characters with unusual materials.

63

Simple Controls and Stringing

Few strings and a simple controller are recommended for beginners. Design a bar that is easy to construct and easy to hold. Use strong thread or fishline for stringing (choose a color that will not show against the backdrop) and practice in front of a mirror, until you can manipulate suitable motions for the character.

These suggestions are offered for 12- to 15-inch puppets. Vary the proportions of the control bars for larger or smaller dolls.

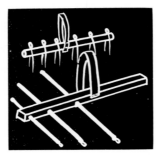

1. SINGLE CONTROL BAR—On a 1″ dowel 12″ long, mark six equally spaced spots and insert screw eyes. Attach leg strings to the first and last screw eyes. Attach hand strings to the second and fifth screw eyes—and the head strings to the third and fourth.

A strong tape can be tacked to this horizontal bar, so the marionette can be hung when not in use.

2. CROSS-SHAPED CONTROL BAR—Use 1″ square white pine about 14″ long, and drill 2 or 3 holes large enough for ½″ dowel crossbars to slide through. Insert half of the dowel and nail or glue each one in place to prevent turning. Insert small screw eyes at each dowel end and tack a loose tape band on top of the pine strip for hanging the control on your arm or on a hook.

3. AIRPLANE-SHAPED CONTROL—Use a long wooden strip, about 1½″ wide and about ½″ thick. Cut 2 six-inch, 1 eight-inch and 1 twelve-inch lengths. Make crossbars of the three short pieces and screw them on top of the 12″ strip. Add screw eyes at both ends of each crossbar.

Any control can have screw eyes added at each end of the long bar for additional strings.

Another 6″ crossbar for the rear legs of an animal marionette can be added to the end of the 12″ strip.

Costumes and Stage

Since each part of a marionette production is an art in itself, these suggestions are offered to the beginner to tempt him to explore each separate field.

As in a painting, try to create a harmonious unit which includes the costumed marionettes, the scenery and the lighting. Study colors under spot, flood and strip lighting to select the most effective for the play.

COSTUMING—Design a costume that identifies the character, yet does not interfere with the movements. Fabrics that fall in soft folds are often preferred for these tiny actors. Seek advice from experienced sewers before and while making costumes.

STAGING—Design an attractive stage that does not detract from the actors. Consider and plan the stage, the curtains, the place for the puppeteers, room for the puppets to hang or be concealed when not in use, the method of lighting and the scenery. Stage properties can be built of various papier-mâché methods.

A simple stage can be made of a large unlidded box set on a strong table. Place the open side against a large frame clamped to the table edge. Plan separate curtains to hide puppeteers and puppets. Saw a large rectangular opening in the top of the box for string action. Try a long vertical slit near the back of each box side. A mural of changing scenes which fits through the slits, can be wound on dowels outside of the box stage.

65

Photograph, courtesy of Greenwich Public Schools, Greenwich, Connecticut.

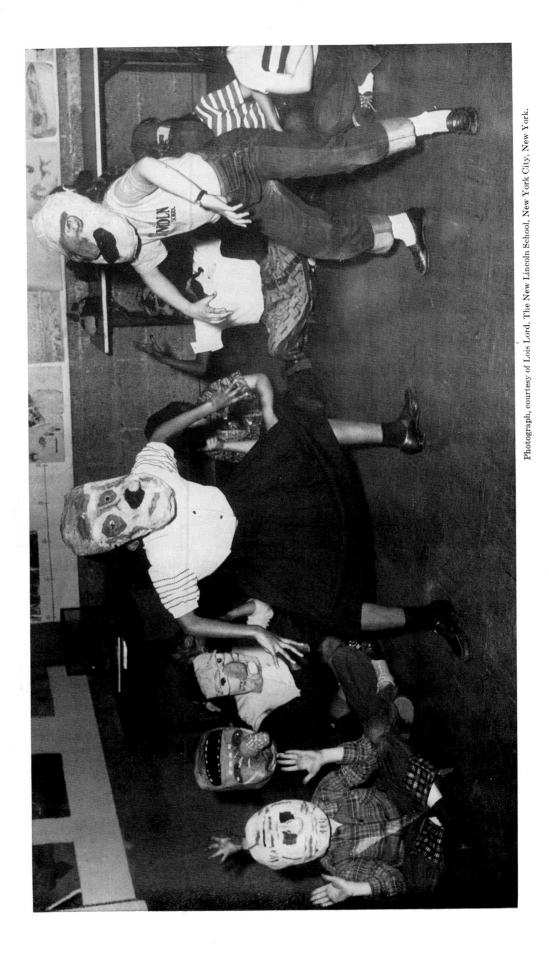

Photograph, courtesy of Lois Lord, The New Lincoln School, New York City, New York.

Chapter Eleven

VARIETY IN MASK MAKING

Essential Materials and Equipment

Newspapers	Novelty Papers	White Paste
Scissors	Paper Plates	Tempera
String	Paper Cups	Brushes
Ruler	Balloons	Nonhardening Clay
Stapler	Cloth	Crayons
Gummed Tape	Trimmings	Bucket and Rags

Mask making has been a recognized art for centuries. In many parts of the world masks were used for religious purposes, in the theatre and for home or building decoration. Since today, as in the past, masks have a popular appeal, mask making is a fine way to stimulate and develop creativity.

Your masks can be inspired or improved by museum trips, films and exhibits. Observe the characteristics of masks made of clay, wood, stone, metals and other materials.

Although many and varied materials have been used for masks, you will find papier-mâché constructions both practical and inexpensive.

This museum piece suggested the use of an inflated balloon taped to cardboard strips, as the core for pasted paper layers. For a mask to cover an actor's head, tape to the balloon a neck band wide enough to slip over a head. Cut out the dry paper shell inside of the neck band.

67

Photograph, courtesy Lilly Osborne, Guatemala City.

PERU

Designing and Construction Aids

Papier-mâché pulp is useful for rough textured masks and for features on masks constructed of pasted paper sheets or strips.

Cloth layers inserted between pasted paper ones will add strength to a papier-mâché mask.

Plaster of Paris, sprinkled between pasted papers, will add stiffness as will a few layers of cloth which have been dipped in liquid starch.

To measure features for a mask to wear, fold a ten-inch paper square in half and place the fold against the center of a face. Mark the position of eyes, brows, nostrils, lips, chin and ears. Cut out the features before unfolding the paper which can be used as a modeling or painting guide.

Use a mirror to help you mark on the folded paper or to observe the position, shape and size of your features. Also use a mirror when painting a self mask.

Another measuring method is to place a slightly damp paper towel or soft cloth over a face. Rub a scrap of soft-colored chalk on the covered features and around the cheek and chin line. Use this as an alternate guide in designing a mask to wear.

Twisted, wadded or coiled newspapers are useful for bold relief modeling. Fasten them to the mask with a few layers of pasted strips.

Torn, cut or sculptured papers can be used for features or for decorative trimmings. Fold, pleat, curl, score and bend many kinds of papers in your exploration. Include flap hinges when adding cut paper parts. The hinges can be pasted on the mask surface or inserted in cut slits and pasted to the under side of the mask.

Facial characteristics can be identified by modeling, by surface treatment, and by a combination of both.

Novelty papers can provide unusual surfaces. Be generous with paste if you want a smooth or secure top layer of paper on the mask.

Use paper towels or other clean light-colored papers for the last pasted layer when you intend to use crayon instead of paint for coloring.

If you have not observed facial construction, close your eyes and feel your face. Notice the parts that sink in or bump out. Feel a cat's face and faces of dogs. Notice the differences.

One activity often leads to another. Try attaching a mask to a hood made of cloth or paper. Hoods are good foundations on which to attach hair, hats and collars.

Save old sheets and dry cleaners' large paper bags for inexpensive costumes. They can be cut, stapled, pasted, or sewn and decorated with crayons or paints.

Apply pasted papers over cores of poultry wire, reed or cartons. Consider using huge papier-mâché masks for parades, for stage or party decorations and tiny ones for dolls, for costume jewelry, or as party favors.

Trimmings are essential in finishing novel and unusual masks. Acquire a collection of discarded or inexpensive materials for the purpose.

Simple Masks of Cardboard, Bags or Boxes

1. From a long pliable cardboard strip, wide and long enough to cover a head, cut out seeing, breathing and speaking holes. Protrud-

69

ing features of cut paper can have flap hinges to simplify the fastening. Some features can be attached to upper and lower edges of the strip or worked into slits in the cardboard.

2. Slip a paper bag over your head and pinch or mark the spots to be cut out. Make slits in the bag to insert cutouts for hair, horns, ears, nose, tongue, whiskers or costume accessories. Staples or paste will hold the additions in place.

3. An empty oatmeal box can have top and bottom removed and be slit along the length. Use the curved surface as a base on which to add features.

4. Shoe and hat boxes with lids taped to the box provide other shapes for mask bases. If part of the lid is untaped and bent away from the box it may suggest an open mouth of a square-jawed creature.

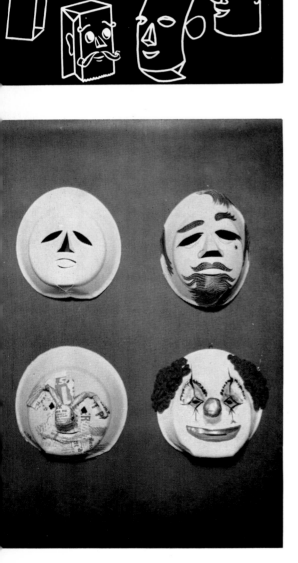

Paper Plate Masks

1. On the back of an eight- or nine-inch paper plate, sketch the position of the features, and cut them out, if the mask is to be worn. Cut two slits, a few inches apart, in the rim. Overlap the slit ends to form a chin and staple them in position. Model features of cut paper or coils and crumpled wads to attach with pasted strips.

2. Soak a paper plate in water for five or ten minutes. On or off a face, gently bend the plate to shape it. Fold, pleat and fasten part of the rim to form a chin or forehead. Use another soaked plate to cut up and model for features. Fasten additions with paste and paper.

70

Masks over Curved Objects

1. Pots, jugs, jars or bowls provide curved shapes on which to construct papier-mâché masks. Cover one side of the object with a layer of wet paper, then add enough layers of pasted dry strips to give a firm, strong thickness. On the paper shell, paste crumpled paper wads for features and facial contours and secure them with pasted strips. When the mask is dry, remove the mold and trim the mask. Overlapping pasted strips will smooth cut edges.

2. Inflated balloons vary in size and shape. Suspend them while working or fasten one on a weighted soda bottle. One side of the balloon can be used as a mold instead of a large jar or build up a face on each side of the balloon. When the paper shell is dry it can be split into two separate masks.

Papier-Mâché Life Masks

Teamwork is recommended when constructing masks on faces to make the experience more enjoyable. Gummed tape will speed the process.

Cover the face with two layers of soft cloth or damp paper towels which have cut holes for eyes and nostrils. Bind one gummed tape strip around the head at the forehead level, and another under the chin and over the top of the head. Vary the direction of the tape in covering the face so that the features will be clearly defined.

Apply three or four layers on the face, lift off the shell and let it dry on a paper wad. On and under the dry mask, add layers of paper and paste. The eyes, nostrils and mouth can be open or closed. Trim and finish all cut edges with overlapping pasted papers.

Masks over Clay Molds

1. Nonhardening modeling clay is often used to model mask bases for papier-mâché. Headdress, hair or collar can be included in the clay model or added later with paste and paper. Use a layer or two of wet paper over the clay before adding the pasted strips.

2. If your supply of clay is limited, start with a firm wad of paper. Model the clay over the wad. Or find an oval rock to use instead of the paper wad.

3. Instead of using the papier-mâché method described for masks over pots and jars and applicable to other molds, try wetting buckram in warm water and press it over a clay mask. When the buckram is dry, lift it off the clay and reinforce it with pasted paper applied on both top and bottom surfaces.

Plaster of Paris Molds for Masks

When a number of papier-mâché reproductions of an original mask are needed, first model a mask of nonhardening clay and coat it with vaseline, baby oil, or liquid soap.

For making a plaster mold add to your materials list: plaster of Paris, a large mixing pan, cold water, and a strong cardboard box a few inches larger and deeper than the mask. Grease the inside of the box.

Spread newspapers to protect furniture and speed the cleaning up process.

Sift the plaster into the pan of cold water while constantly stirring the mixture. Try equal parts of plaster and water, or sift the plaster, without stirring, until a peak appears above the water. Then stir until the mixture has the consistency of thick gravy. Lay the mask, face up in the box, and slowly pour the plaster until it is an inch or two above the mask. Sometimes gentle taps on the box sides will eliminate air bubbles and level the plaster.

Let the mold dry before removing the box or the clay mask.

Plaster of Paris molds show clear definitions of the clay features. To preserve the characteristics in a paper mask, use one or two layers of soft wet paper before adding pasted newspaper layers. Tear the paper in pieces small enough to fit into the indentations. Six to ten pasted layers usually make a firm paper shell. When the paper mask is dry, lift it from the mold, trim the edges and cover the top of the mask and the edges with a layer or two of pasted strips.

Pariscraft*, a bandage impregnated with Plaster of Paris powder, is useful in making or strengthening masks and other papier-mâché objects. Just cut a section off the roll, dip in water, and smooth or model it over the paper shell.

*For information, please write to Johnson & Johnson, New Brunswick, N. J. or the following suppliers:
J. L. Hammett Co., Union, N. J.; Lyons, N. Y.; Kendall Sq., Cambridge, Mass.
Practical Drawing Co., Box 5388, Dallas 22, Texas.
St. Paul Book & Stationery Co., Corner Sixth and Cedar, St. Paul 1, Minnesota.
H. S. Crocker Co., Inc., 720 Mission St., San Francisco 1, California.

Papier-mâché Toys from Mexico.

Chapter Twelve

TOYS AND GAMES

Materials and Equipment

Newspaper	Stapler	Seeds
Boxes	Gummed tape	Beads
Tubes	Paper fasteners	Feathers
Cans	Needle	Fabrics
Bottles	Thread	Yarn
Paper plates	Scissors	Sponges
Paper cups	Nails	Twigs
Novelty papers	Hammer	Balloons
Egg cartons	Wire	Gourds
Wooden boxes	Elastic bands	Pebbles
Storage bags	Cup hooks	Bells
Storage boxes	Jar rings	Flexible poles
Spools	Mat knife	Springs
Scrap wood	Cement	Hoops
Dowels	Paste	Crayons
Paints	Brushes	Nonhardening clay
String	Beans	

Many years ago, toys showed the way of life; the traditions, the legends and products of each locality. Recently, transportation and the free interflow of cultures have affected all forms of folk art, including toymaking.

The study of historical folk toys aids in understanding nations and localities. Books, films, slides, museum field trips and group discussion will all contribute to the study and activity, whether toymaking is for play or for a profession.

Toys and games are often creations of feeling, rather than reason. There should be no restrictions in exploration and no criticism of any application that serves a student's purpose.

Preparations and presentations can be simplified, if activities have general classifications. Let these divisions suggest other descriptive classifications:

> Rhythm Instruments
> Toys for Make-believe
> Miniatures and Models
> Motion Toys
> Play and Practice Games
> Decorative Toys
> Miscellaneous Toys

Rhythm Instruments

DRUMS—Strengthen large open cylinders with pasted paper layers and decorate. Make drumheads of closely woven fabric or window shades. Pad twigs or dowels with pasted paper for drumsticks.

MARACAS AND RATTLES—Put some rice, beans or pebbles in a small box and insert a smooth stick handle. Seal the box and fasten the handle to the box with pasted paper strips. Cans covered with pasted papers, paper shells made over fruits, vegetables, clay or balloons, provide a wide variety of shapes for rattles.

76

TAMBOURINES—Paper shells, made over clay models or over dishes can be trimmed and strung with bells and ribbons. Several paper plates, pasted together and covered with a pasted layer of toweling can have a rim border of punched holes. Pop bottle tops with nail holes can be attached to the rim with paper clips.

BELL BRACELETS—Rims of small plates, rope covered with pasted paper, slices of oatmeal cartons can all have bells attached.

HORNS, FLUTES, BUGLES—Insert whistles in the mouthpiece of cones or tubes. Add a bugle handle of wire or rope, covered with paper.

GONGS—Cover one side of a tin tray, pot lid or pie plate with paste and paper. Punch two holes near the rim for a cord handle. Pad one end of a metal rod. Use either end for striking. Add gay decorations with crayons or water paints on the paper-covered side.

Toys for Make-believe

COSTUME HATS—Use boxes, paper clips and plates, and cardboard of different weights to construct the hats. Staple the sections together, then cover the hat with a few layers of pasted paper.

COSTUMES—Find suitable cartons to combine for costumes for special storybook characters. Combine carton parts of costumes with fabric parts when needed. Use staples, gummed paper tape, adhesive tape and pasted layers for the carton costumes.

HOBBY HORSES—Large animal heads modeled of pulp or paper wads over tubes and boxes, can be attached to broomsticks with tacks and gummed tape.

77

PULL TOYS—Any figure or animal construction described in preceding chapters can be placed in or attached to toy carts. With wire, attach wheels of cardboard or spools to strong boxes to make a pull cart.

BOX PUPPETS—Crayon or small cereal boxes can be stapled to fabric sleeves for box puppets. Model features and strengthen the box with paste-covered paper.

MASKS—Consult Chapter 11 for many ways of making masks. Plan a comfortable fit when they are to be worn for acting or dancing.

PUPPETS AND MARIONETTES—Make a "theatre in the square" by draping a card table with a crayon-decorated sheet. Work hand puppets in stage openings on all four sides. A string puppet can be suspended in an open box. Cut cross-slots in the box sides to work the strings beyond the box stage. Place an animal marionette on a strong box lid. Cut slots in the platform and let a jaw or tail string dangle through the slot. Pull the string for action.

Miniatures and Models

BUILDINGS—Boxes, tubes and scrap cardboard can be assembled for many buildings from simple homes to beautiful cathedrals. Use sandpaper, corrugated and other textured papers for the last pasted layers to give variety in surface finishes.

ENGINES, PLANES, CARS, BOATS—Combine boxes and tubes, or if you wish, make a nonhardening clay model. When clay is used, cover the model with one layer of wet paper and six to ten layers of pasted paper. Split the dry paper shell, remove the clay and paste the halves together.

PUPPET STAGES AND STAGE PROPERTIES—Select a suitable carton for the stage. Model some "props" of pulp or paper wads. Use hollow objects for others.

DOLL FURNITURE—Cut away sections of tubes, containers, egg cartons to design miniature furniture. Frames of pop sticks or firm wire can support some furniture parts. Reinforce the miniatures with pasted layers of strong wrapping paper. Several coats of shellac will protect the paint and strengthen the craft.

TOTEM POLES, ROCKETS, LOGS—Slender tubes or firm coils of rolled paper will get you started. Try cardboard scraps for auxiliary parts.

Motion Toys

FLYERS—Paste eight layers of dry newspapers together to make a thick moist pad. Cut out birds, fish, butterflies, or planes and bend the paper to suggest movement. Fasten the dry cutouts with string to one end of a flexible pole.

BOUNCERS—Use discarded springs or make some of strong wire. Fasten a papier-mâché figure on the coil. String and suspend the figure for bouncing action. Try lightweight hollow bodies and arms and legs of paper folds for other bouncing toys.

ROLLING TOYS—Pulp beads strung on wires add appeal to large hoops. Hit the hoop with a

79

smoothly sanded dowel. Insert beans in a cylindrical carton and add a long wire handle attached to allow free revolving action. Roll the toy on the floor or fasten the handle to a crib or play pen. A year-old baby can use his toes to make the cylinder spin.

ROCKING TOYS—Any papier-mâché figure can be attached to a rocking platform. Be sure that the rockers are strong enough to hold the weight of the figure. Use strong cardboard cylinders or wood, if necessary, for a rocking platform. Push a dowel through wet pulp objects, or through padded or hollow figures. Rest the dowel on forked branches stuck in a base of clay or pulp.

MOBILES—Use the layer method described for flying toys and model free form, abstract or naturalistic shapes to string for mobile action.

Play and Practice Games

RING TOSS—These can be made with any papier-mâché method, as long as there is an extension to act as a catch for the rings. Reinforce the protruding part with wire or cardboard to keep the catch from breaking.

CATCH GAMES—Attach wooden sticks to any hollow shape that is not too large to handle. Fasten the handle to the cup with alternate layers of pasted cloth and paper, which are also useful for making a stronger cup. The ball can be a wad of paper covered with rubber bands. Tie one end of a yard-long cord to the ball and another to the handle. A two-in-one game can be made by extending the wooden dowel above as well as below the cup. Tie a second cord to the handle with a bracelet ring at the opposite end.

BOWLING—Weighted figures of tubes trimmed with yarn or tenpins made of pulp which has been modeled on wooden cores will not break easily if a tennis ball is used by the bowler.

PITCHING—Place a large carton, open end down and reinforce it with gummed tape. Paint a giant size face on each of the four sides and when the paint is dry, cut out holes to permit pitching games with beanbags, buttons or beans. Plan sizes that can be nested to save storage space.

Decorative Toys

BANKS—Milk containers, tubes, or boxes can be modeled with paper wads and pasted strips. Combine cartons for unusual banks and, if you wish, cut a coin slot in each section.

SHADOW BOXES—Relief pictures of pulp or pasted wads and strips can be arranged in a cardboard or wooden box. Yarn, sponges, beads and other collage materials can be used with papier-mâché. Perhaps collections of natural materials can be displayed in your shadow box. Cover the opening with cellophane to make it dustproof.

COSTUME DOLLS—Make a wire core of the figure and nail the feet to a wooden base. Pad the figure with soft paper and wrap it with string. Use scrap fabrics, felt, lace and other trimmings for some of the costumes, and pasted paper for others.

81

Use pop bottles or pop cans for other cores. Add heads of light bulbs, styrofoam, paper wads or paper pulp. Try twisted paper for arms, braided cloth or yarn, or wire. Cover the entire figure with pasted strips before adding a painted costume, or a cloth one.

Refer to solid and hollow figures for other constructions. Perhaps suggestions in the marionette chapter will offer appealing ways of making dolls.

Try tiny ones for lapel ornaments or giants for displays or parades.

KATCINA DOLLS—Let strong tubes or fat rolls of newspaper be the cores for ceremonial dolls. Hollow dolls can be turned into banks by cutting a coin slot in the tube.

Miscellaneous Toys

SURPRISE TOY—Wrap small toys and candies separately with waxed paper, then together with dry strips of tissue or crepe paper. Bunch the toys together as you wrap them to form a

Four Hopi Katcina dolls such as are actually used by the Hopi Indians in their ceremonies. Katcina represent Hopi divinities and are carved in wood and elaborately colored with paint.

ball or egg shape. Bind the dry strips with a layer of pasted strips and add gay decorations with paint, ribbons, and sparkle.

Soft Ball—Crumple paper to shape a firm ball and cover the paper with a large square of strong cloth. Twist the cloth at the top of the ball and add a string tie. Crayon a face and use the loose cloth corners to suggest hair, or a headdress.

Balloon Toys—Inflated balloons covered with six or eight pasted layers of paper can be painted as globes. Different sizes and shapes of inflated balloons, fastened together and then completely covered with pasted paper layers will look like creatures from Never-Never Land.

Toys to Ride—Fasten a crumpled paper head to a box or barrel with several layers of gummed tape. Nail on legs of wood. Model a saddle of bent cardboard.

Build animals by combining and attaching hollow cardboard cartons. Shape others of poultry wire. Put a "lazy creature" on a rocking platform or on one with wheels so that it can be pushed or pulled.

Make animals perform by constructing only bodies and heads. Let your legs, and those of a friend, provide action for these moving toys.

Stuffed Animals—Draw and cut out an animal of double thickness brown wrapping paper. Fold in edges and sew or staple the two sides together. Leave an opening for a stuffing of crumpled paper or cloth. Strengthen the edges and the animal with pasted paper patches. Try printed papers for decorative accents or add features and textures with crayons and paint.

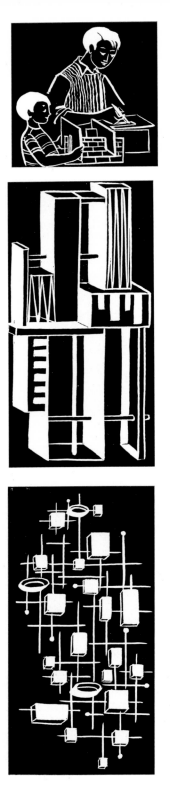

BLOCKS FOR PLAY AND DISPLAY—For the very young, block play provides exercise and encourages social development. For all ages, boxes of varied sizes and shapes can whet imaginations. Join some together with tape or glue, stack others without fasteners so their use can be changed as ideas change.

One need may require doors or windows on a carton, another—a stone or brick pattern. These designs, executed with crayons, paint or colored papers, can motivate new play action or display purpose.

Cut narrow grooves in cardboard walls to permit interlocking. Combine these walls with cartons in blockbuilding activities. Encourage students to initiate and organize their own projects. Feel free to combine other papier-mâché objects with blocks as ideas are put to use. Crumpled paper foliage glued to twigs, models of trains, cars, people or animals—all widen the scope of action.

Use wire, reed or cord to thread boxes for decorative panels, stabiles or mobiles. A surface coat of metallic papers will reflect light. Paper mosaics can be cut from colored papers or gay magazine advertisements. Heavy applications of paint or crayons can cover soil or print. Remember that the apparent weight of the boxes in the construction can be affected by the color values of the surface decoration.

Assemble cartons, grooved cardboard, mailing tubes and dowels of rolled paper. Discuss new sources for materials and new uses for varied sizes and shapes. Consider stacking and storage suggestions. Review the many activities that are motivated or aided by block constructions.

84

Let the ideas in this chapter suggest other uses for toy or game objects of papier-mâché. Bead-trimmed hoops can be party decorations or mobile and stabile sections. Catch games can be tree ornaments; sewn animals, unstuffed, can be masks or party hats. Use your initiative and create other crafts to fill a particular requirement.

Photograph, courtesy of Marion Quin Dix, Elizabeth, New Jersey.

Chapter Thirteen

GIFTS AND DISPLAY

Essential Materials and Equipment

Paper: Newspaper, towels, crepe, tissue, colored construction, lace doilies, paper napkins, cellophane.

Cardboard: Scraps, tubes, boxes, large cartons.

Cores: Bottles, cans, stones, balloons, wire, dowels, reed, rope, lids, poultry wire, scrap wood, plywood, wooden spatulas, pipe cleaners, corks, lampshades.

Fasteners: String, gummed tape, paste, household cement, toothpicks, staples, pin and earring backs, clip clothespins, liquid papier-mâché.*

Tools: Scissors, nails, hammer, wire cutters, measuring tape, pins, needle, thread, stapler, pliers, palette knife.

Supplies: Paints, crayons, brushes, clear finishing varnish, denatured alcohol, papier-mâché compound, plastic spray, nonhardening clay, colloid-treated fabric, plaster of Paris, crinoline, liquid starch, paste pan, aluminum foil, plaster bandage.

Trimmings: Yarn, fabrics, beads, flowers, natural materials, candies, sponges, sequins, fringes.

Papier-mâché experiences develop resourcefulness. Art for fun can lead to serious jobs which also offer incentives for learning. Seeing new things, experimenting with new materials, with new processes and their applications, will provide discoveries to contribute to daily living.

*For information about lacquer base and vinyl base papier-mâché, please write The Plasti-Glaze Company, 11457 114th Avenue, Youngstown, Arizona.

To be a creative craftsman with papier-mâché, be sincere. Consider structural design or shape as you create. Decorative design, or what goes on the surface, should be in keeping with the shape. Sensitivity to design is acquired, not by memorizing rules, but by the continuous process of creative activity.

Holders

Holders are practical gifts. Plan sizes and shapes that are suitable for dried grasses, letters, wastepaper, pencils, string, candy, cookies, sewing equipment, candles, jewelry and other articles. When fresh flowers or leaves are used, place a container for water in the holder.

Easy-to-make holders can have, as starting bases, discarded containers which formerly held frozen foods, cheeses, milk, juices, salt, cereals, spices or cosmetics. Change the shapes by combining them, by adding handles, by modeling with pulp or crumpled paper or by adding bold relief with rope. The new shapes can be attached to the container with pasted paper layers.

Spread paste on a long strip of corrugated cardboard. Roll it tightly and squeeze the roll for a varied shape. The roll may need a strong tie or a weight on one section to hold it in position while the paste dries. For more variety, fasten two or more rolls together with pasted paper strips. Use the holder for pencils, crayons, brushes, or dried grasses.

Make a smooth pulp of soft tissue paper mixed with plenty of paste. Spread the mixture with a palette knife on boxes of wood or cardboard. While the pulp is still wet, imbed arrangements of yarn. Try stamping recessed designs in the moist pulp with nonabsorbent tools or add surface decorations of seeds, fish scales and other natural materials.

Twist and bend a wire lampshade frame into a new shape. Cover the armature with a few layers of moist plaster bandage. Build up surface designs by modeling moist bandage on a dry undercoat or fasten rope modeling to the container surface with pieces of wet bandage.

Design a solid form of nonhardening clay. Cover it with one wet paper layer, then six or more dry pasted layers. If the shape permits, lift off the dry shell; trim and finish the cut edges. When necessary, split the shell to remove the clay.

Pariscraft* plaster bandage on a re-shaped lampshade.

Use the same process over a glass, china or plastic mold, but change the shape by adding bases, or handles, or by fastening several papier-mâché shells together. Jar lids, circular boxes, wire, cord, pipe cleaners and other articles can be added to the bowl with pasted paper strips. Adhesive tape, used under the pasted strips, will simplify adding handles to the papier-mâché dish. Make a covered dish by using a matching shell for the lid. Paste a cardboard strip on the inner rim of the bottom shell. Let part of the strip extend above the shell.

Holders for letters or clippings can be made by pasting paper coils on the edges of a heavy cardboard base. Woven trays need warp and weft strips of thick folded newspaper. Add paste to the last fold to strengthen and stiffen the strip and tuck in all raw paper edges.

Cut a circle, oval, square, rectangle or free form from a pad made of six or more news-

*Please refer to page 73 for Pariscraft information.

89

paper sheets which have been pasted together. Shape the cut pad with your hands or over a box, can or rock. Fashion it as you wish with pleats, folds or cut openings. Support the drying form in a fabric hammock or in a bed of aluminum foil. Try a string tie to prop the shell while it dries.

Cover a dish or bowl with a layer of cellophane or aluminum foil. Add layers of stretched crepe paper, brushing paste between each layer. Alternate the grain to record the coverage. Gently stamp nailheads, erasers, or sticks on the moist shell for a textured surface. Make a pulp of crepe paper flakes and paste for relief modeling on the dry shell.

Photograph, courtesy of Wm. H. Milliken, Jr.

To make candle holders, cement rings cut from mailing tubes which have a hole to fit the average candle, to dry flower or foliage forms which have been cut from a pad of pasted paper sheets and modeled while damp. Tie or support raised petals while they are drying. When several pads of petals or leaves are made for a holder, paint each pad separately before cementing them together.

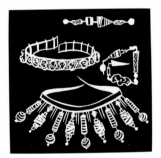

Costume Jewelry

Papier-mâché miniature masks, figures, flowers, and holders can be worn as decorative lapel pins. Collect small corks, hairpins, pipe cleaners, paper clips, toothpicks and tiny glass or plastic vials, to use as cores.

90

Paper beads have many uses. Make them of fine pulp modeled over a wire which makes a hole for stringing and at the same time provides a handle while the pulp is being dried or painted. Other beads can be made of strips or long triangles cut from drawing paper. Spread paste generously on one side of the strip and wind it tightly around a wire.

Be original in your use of paper beads. Combine them with pearls, buttons, scrap felt, yarn or scraps of leather. String or sew them to upholstery fringes. Cement beads on wire to keep them in desired positions.

Tiny masks of pulp or of crumpled wads of paste-covered cleansing tissue modeled on a split cork or on a cardboard base can be made gay with trimmings of wire or feathers. You may need a hairpin or orange stick to model small features. Cement a hatpin or safety pin to the back of the mask.

Lapel vases of papier-mâché to hold small strawflowers can be made of pulp or of strips pasted over a paper tube. Use a plastic or glass vial, instead of a paper tube core to hold water and fresh flowers.

Nuggets made of soft paper which has been covered with paste and crumpled can be painted gold or with color to resemble uncut stones. Cement them to pin or earring backs or wrap them with strands of fine wire for bracelets or necklaces.

Small birds also can be modeled of crumpled paste-covered paper. You may wish to trim one with bits of real feathers and glamorize another with a coat of sequins.

Butterflies, flowers and foliage can be cut from six layers of cloth and paper pasted in alternate layers. Clip or pin these ornaments to place cards and let them serve as party favors.

Dress pipe cleaner dolls with papier-mâché costumes or use the pipe cleaners as cores for pulp modeling.

Accessories for the Home

Papier-mâché pulp and strip methods are applicable for many household needs. Let these suggestions challenge your ingenuity:

1. Repair jewelry, frames, furniture.

2. Cover stones and bricks for doorstops and book ends.

3. Use cigar boxes for sewing equipment or jewelry.

4. Model over sand-filled bottles to use as lamp bases.

5. Wire or string wooden spatulas and paper beads for hot-dish pads.

6. Make decorative bottle stoppers by running a heavy wire through a cork. Let the wire extend above the cork. Model paper on the wire core.

7. Trim hollow cones of window screening for patio food covers.

8. Strengthen paper plates and cardboard containers with gesso. Apply additional coats of gesso for thickness and firmness.

9. Make lightweight shelves of coat hangers and cardboard.

10. Build screen panels of wood. Fill in the frames with a mesh design of wire or reed. Cover all or part of the mesh with pasted paper.

Decorations

Ornaments for tables, doors, mantles or Christmas trees can be used many times in many ways. They can be fragile or sturdy, temporary or permanent. Even fragile creations can be packed carefully and saved for future occasions. Think about the purpose when planning your papier-mâché construction.

Decorative wreathes and sprays can be gay headgear, door trimmings, table centerpieces or garlands for costume accessories. For the core, braid long privet stems, bend coat hangers, shape reed or use discarded hoops and barrel rims. Make other backings of chicken wire, heavy cardboard, plastic foam or plywood.

Draw on manila paper, original patterns for flowers, leaves, bells, fruits, birds, butterflies or figures. Trace around them on a single sheet of unprinted newspaper. Paste this sheet on top of six or eight pasted newspaper sheets and carefully cut out the outlined patterns.

Model the cutouts while the paper is moist. Let them dry before attaching them to the hoop with wire, string, gummed tape or staples. Combine the modeled paper cutouts with trimmings of pine cones, nuts, holiday ornaments, feathers or ribbons. Add gay color with paint, and on some try sparkling accents of soap flakes, sequins, beads, cellophane straws or wire-wrapped bits of broken colored glass.

Let paper plates of varied sizes and shapes be your motivating material. Explore their decorative possibilities for creating masks, amusing toy-like figures, puppet stage properties, fans, stabiles and mobiles.

Hold two matching plates, face to face and staple, sew or lace the rims together. Do they suggest tree ornaments, banks, or doll heads? Cut a slit in a third plate and fit it on the two. Do you see a hat, a collar, or a stand for the stapled plates?

Score a plate and fold it. Can you use a thick semicircle as part of another construc-

93

tion? Do paper cup additions whet your imagination?

Try cutouts of paper plates or folded and sculptured papers for features, body sections or costumes. Insert them in slits and paste the inserted ends to the plates, or staple the cutouts to the plate surface.

Punch holes in paper plates or cutouts and connect them with wool ties. Do these suggest marionettes?

Model faces of paper pulp or of wads and pasted strips on the raised section of the backs of paper plates. Use them separately as over-mantle decorations or fasten a row of masks on a wide tape to trim a door.

Strengthen all paper plate inventions with a few layers of pasted paper. Suspend the decorations or fasten them to bases of clay, pulp, wood or plaster of Paris.

Heavy cardboard or plywood cutouts can be made plump with relief modeling of paper pulp or wads, held in place with pasted strips. Sawdust, excelsior or crayon shavings patted into moist pulp, colored pulp made with confetti or torn flakes of colored comics or wrinkled sheets of paste-covered papers can make the models more appealing. Add an easel back, if you wish; fix a stand or suspend the craft. Decorations which will be seen from all sides can be built up on both front and back.

Egg dividers from cartons or crates, apple dividers and other pressed pulp papers can be cut apart in various sizes and assorted shapes. Staple two or more together for an ornament. Speed your color work by dipping the ornament in one paint color and spattering on the other colors. Feature your favorite constructions with brushwork or sparkling accents. Use

94

waxed paper as a table cover while the wet paint is drying to keep the ornaments from sticking. Or add paper-clip hooks and hang them on a line to dry.

Egg-divider ornaments are gay on Christmas trees. They can be containers for small gifts, floral centerpieces, wrappings for Easter eggs, napkin holders, place cards, nut cups, and costume accessories for dolls and puppets. Turn some of the ornaments into papier-mâché figures by combining them with paper coils and wads, with yarn, with cellophane straws or with plastic foam. You will find egg and apple dividers helpful when designing mobile and stabile constructions. Link them to cut sections of paper plates in some of your explorations.

Decorative Figures

Nonhardening oil-clay figures, or oil clay modeled over cores of firm paper wads, wood scraps, corks, small stones or bottles can be made permanent by covering the clay with one layer of aluminum foil and several layers of pasted paper. Sometimes scrap wire, pipe cleaners or strong cardboard are needed to support extensions. The use of scrap material cores often suggests a figure and also makes your clay supply go farther.

Paper pulp bottle protectors are provoking. The pulp can be slightly bent or slit to make deeper indentations. Cut the neck off the protector; fit it in the opening at an angle for further stimulation. Model a head of oil clay or of paper wads over part of the pulp neck. Cover the clay with aluminum foil, then several pasted paper layers. Add arms, legs, wings or

95

costumes with layers of pasted paper over supports of wire or reed.

Bend a wire coat hanger into an outline of a figure. Connect several hangers for larger figures or for more intricate ones. Clip sections of hangers for short pieces. Fasten separate wire sections together with adhesive tape, pipe cleaners or fine wire strands. Cover the wire frame with pasted paper. Feel free to wrap gummed tape around the frame, or bind it with rag strips before a pasted paper coat is applied. Large wire frames can be covered first with a filler of poultry wire or window screening before paper layers are applied.

Utilize dry and damp reed strands which lend themselves to graceful curves. The flexibility of reed will help you create. Tape or tie the shape in position and partially fill a large frame by weaving damp strands under and over the frame as you cross the opening. Cut newspaper sheets a bit smaller than the frame and paste them on one or both sides of the woven reed within the frame.

When hollow frames are covered, cut the paper a bit larger, add paste to the paper edge and fasten the excess border over the reed. Pleat the fullness, or clip the border and let one flap overlap another. Apply as many pasted layers as you need and alternate sides as you add each layer.

Review Chapters 5, 6, 7 and 8 for other solid and hollow figure construction methods. Decorative figures are applicable for many practical purposes. Their uses range from tiny ones for place cards to huge ones for floats, parades, store windows and other display objectives.

Photograph, courtesy of Ellery L. Gibson,
Arizona State College, Flagstaff, Arizona.

Commercial Displays

Papier-mâché compound, a dry fine powder, is used by doll doctors, taxidermists and other display artists. Mix the powder with enough wet paste to hold the fine pulp together. Model solid objects or work over a poultry wire core which has been wrapped with brown gummed paper. The mixture can be applied and modeled with a palette knife and clay modeling tools, as well as with the fingers. When dry, it can be carved and sandpapered, and stained or painted with opaque colors.

Papier-mâché compound, when mixed with paste, looks and feels like plastic wood. The dry models are strong and durable. Display figures can change character, if the original model is carved, or if new features or costumes are built up with more of the compound mixture.

Photograph, courtesy of Marion Quin Dix, Elizabeth, N. J.

Pariscraft bas-relief by John Resh, a participant in the Creative Art Education Workshop, Rutgers University S.S., New Brunswick, N. J.

graph, courtesy of Ford Museum, Dearborn, Michigan. Designer, Louis Reynal.

Designed and executed by Richard Rush Studios, Chicago, Illinois.

Sculpt-o-fab*, a colloid-treated fabric, available in several weights, is utilized as papier-mâché is utilized, by many display artists. The fabric must be dipped in a special solvent to make it obey the artist. When partially dry, it can be modeled like pasted paper layers. When wet with solvent, strips or pieces can be applied over any mold which has been completely covered with aluminum foil.

Even a display of one thickness is strong and weatherproof when dry. The gray color of the dry display piece can be covered with opaque paint and protected when necessary, with a coat of clear lacquer.

Plastex*, a plaster impregnated cloth, when dipped in or brushed with water, becomes soft and pliable. It is easily modeled and dries quickly. A strong surfacing material for objects of foamed plastics, it is equally useful as a cover for wire armatures.

Window screening sandwiched between a few layers of pasted paper makes a sturdy yet flexible pad useful for speedy display work.

*For Sculpt-o-fab or Plastex information, please write to Ben Walters, Inc., 11 West 20th Street, New York 11, New York.

First cut a paper pattern to use as a guide. Cut paper layers a bit larger than the wire. Place the mesh cutout between the paper ones, then staple all three together at the edges. Use a stapler to hold twists and turns in place or catch them with a needle threaded with strong thread or fine wire.

Construct mobile parts or wire sculptures with sheets or strips of paper-covered screening. The paper is a protection from cut wire ends and also provides a surface for water-soluble paints. Let this experience lead to combinations of mesh wire and fabrics, yarn, ribbons and other materials.

Mass production of displays brings in the use of molds of plaster of Paris, rubber and other materials. Discoveries for speeding or improving constructions are welcomed by display firms, who encourage artists to create new ways of working and new designs.

Eye-catching color, new materials, and unusual trimming treatments must all be considered and utilized by display artists. Papier-mâché offers a challenging stimulus to the imagination and insists on creativity. Its applicability includes the educational, recreational, fine and commercial art fields.

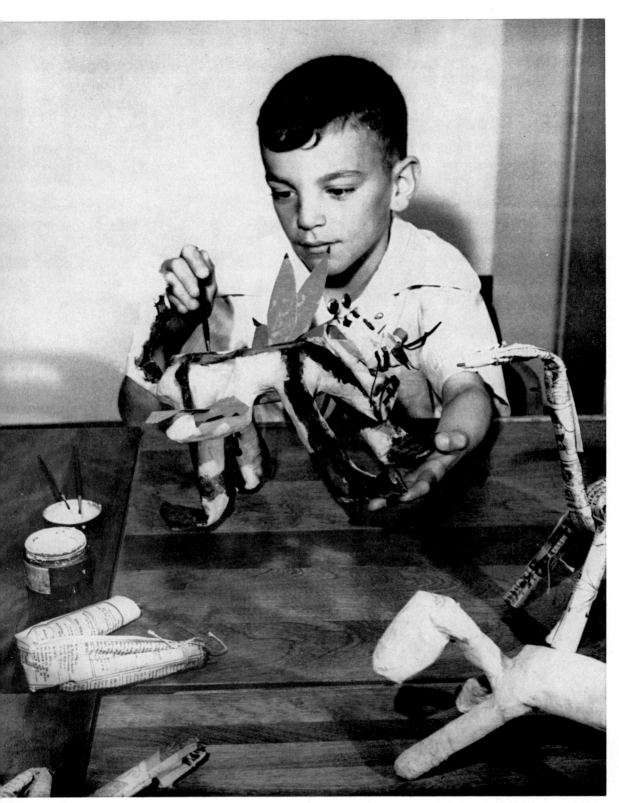

Photograph, courtesy of Tucson Public Schools, Tucson, Arizona

Chapter Fourteen

SURFACE DESIGN AND COLOR

In the preceding chapters, the variety of suggestions for papier-mâché activities are intended as beginnings—to stimulate your ingenuity and to challenge you to express your own ideas with many discarded or inexpensive materials.

The structural design you construct is part of your plan. The surface treatment, or decorative design, should belong to the structure and should not affect the function of the craft.

Study good examples to develop design and color sensitivity. Read approved books on design to grow in understanding. Learn to organize basic design elements, line, form, color, texture, space, to achieve harmony.

Think about your papier-mâché construction. What special quality do you wish to accent through surface treatment?

Heavy or light.
Shiny or dull.
Smooth or rough.
Strong or fragile.
Still or mobile.
Realistic or fantastic.

You will have time to think, to plan and to collect materials while the papier-mâché craft is drying. The size of the object, the construction method and weather affect the drying time. Sunlight or infrared heat lamps will speed drying as will radiators and other heat outlets. When the paper is dry and when you know what you wish to show you are ready to add surface design and color. Be sure of your idea and aim for technical skill in expressing it.

101

Very young children are often satisfied with simple direct painting on papier-mâché. Older ones may wish to make trial color sketches to avoid disappointment. Students of all ages can profit by experiments with many materials to develop confidence and skill in decorative design.

For a simple approach, limit your experiments to one medium or one material.

Exploring Paper

Materials:

White and colored drawing papers, corrugated cardboard, colored magazine pages, comic sheets, foreign newspapers, cancelled stamps, lace doilies, confetti, labels, gummed seals, notebook reinforcements, cellophane, crepe paper, wallpaper, gift wrappings, greeting cards, seed envelopes, catalogues, gummed tapes, painted and crayonned papers.

Experiments:

Select from paper, pleasing color or texture areas. Cut, tear or sculpture them. Pin, staple or paste the papers to the papier-mâché article.

Exploring Fabric and Yarn

Materials:

Scraps of plain and printed fabrics of cotton, silk, plastics or wool; flocking, em-

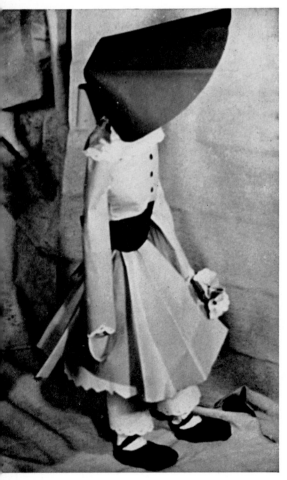

102

broidery, felt, artificial flowers, gloves, socks, ribbons, tapes, string, rope, woolen yarns.

Experiments:

Paste cut or torn strips or patches of fabric. Sew a slipcover or tack a cover with pins or staples. Bind a construction with string or yarn or make line arrangements on a tacky cement or shellac surface. Pin or staple heavy cords to the surface of the construction. Dip string in tempera colored paste or shellac and drop it on the surface. Let it fall as it will or guide the movement of the string. When fabric or yarn is used for a partial covering, first apply a background coat of paint or a pasted layer of selected paper.

Exploring Nature

Materials:

Seeds, shells, bark, grasses, cornhusks, reed, dried leaves, berries, popcorn, straw flowers, raffia, twigs, feathers, fish scales, moss, pine cones, cocoanut fibre, milkweed silk, shavings, sawdust, wood chips.

Experiments:

Pin, paste or cement the materials. Imbed them when necessary. Use natural materials for a textured surface or for emphasis in one section only.

103

Exploring Metal

Materials:

Poultry mesh wire, window screening, clock and watch parts, paper clips, nails, tacks, copper wire, aluminum foil, thin tin and copper sheets, clothes hangers, plastic and cloth-covered wires.

Photograph, courtesy of Wm. H. Milliken, Jr.

Experiments:

Draw upon the knowledge gained from core construction experiences with wire or metal mesh. Work with a material and let it help you. Use tin snips and pliers for cutting and bending. Wear gloves, when necessary, to protect your hands. Paint the construction first if you need a background for the wire decoration.

104

Discovering Design

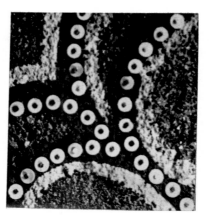

Some Source Materials:

String, wire, matches, washers, rubber bands, buttons, paper clips, hooks, cut and torn papers, hairpins and safety pins, notebook reinforcements, shells, pebbles, seaweed, leaves, grasses, twigs, seeds.

Experiments:

Consider line, form, space, texture and contrast as you repeat the arrangements in vertical, horizontal or diagonal directions for rhythm. Vary the sizes of materials which are combined and space them carefully for a balanced design.

Record an arrangement by repeating it on a tacky shellac-covered surface.

Discover a suitable texture or pattern to stimulate stencil, brush or crayon work on papier-mâché objects.

105

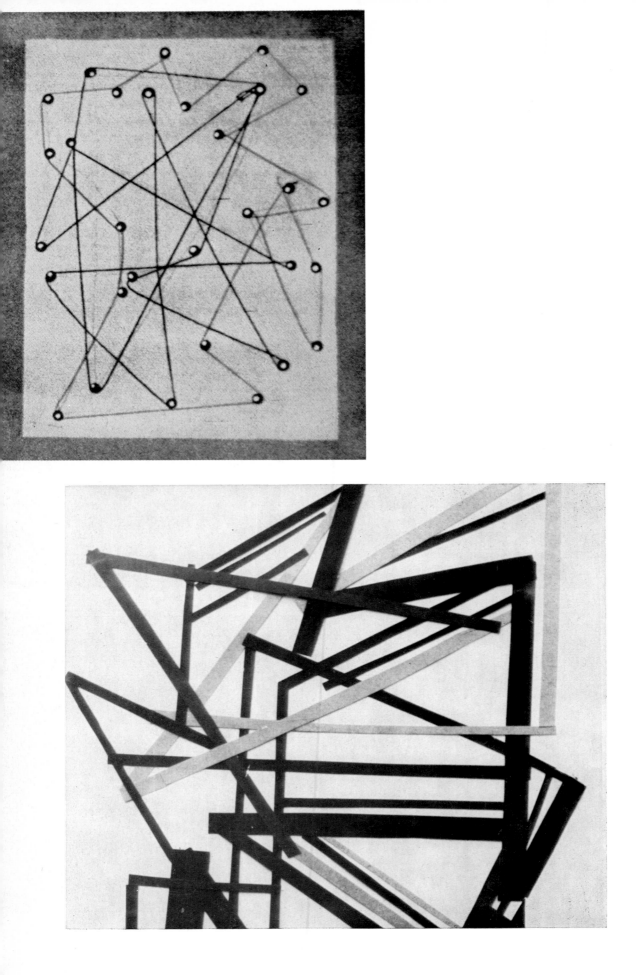

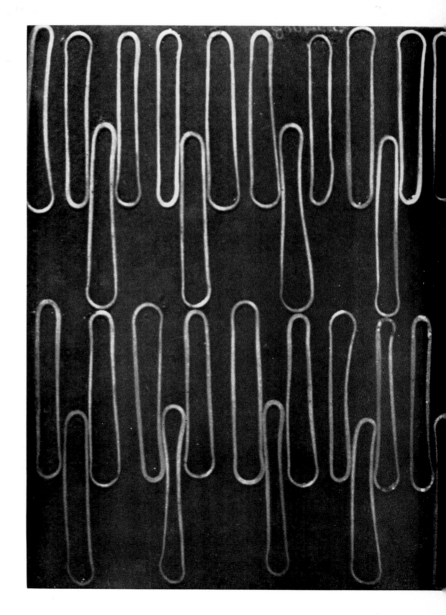

Crafts, courtesy of Binney & Smith Inc.; photograph, courtesy of McCall's Children's Annual, Volume I.

Exploring Paints

Paints:

Tempera—a wet opaque paint, soluble in water.

Powder Paint—dry colors, mix with water for use.

Water Colors—semi-moist pans of transparent color.

Finger Paint—ready-mixed, soluble in water.

Finger Paint—dry colors, mix with water for use with hands or tools.

Enamels—opaque paints, soluble in turpentine.

Oil Paints—in tubes or cans, soluble in turpentine.

Rubber-based Paints—soluble in water.

Metallic Paints—follow directions on container.

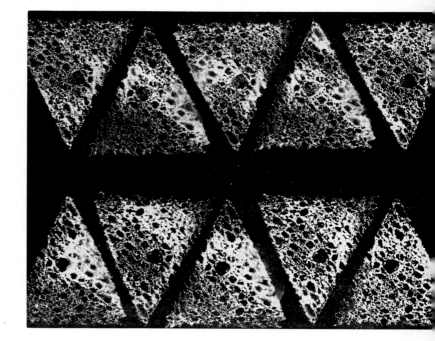

Tempera colors and powder paints are preferred for home and school use.

Painting Tools:

Brushes—camel's-hair, sable, bristle. Clean carefully after use.

Sponges, feathers, cotton swabs, brayers.

Spatter Tools:

Spray guns, airbrush, toothbrush and spatula or wire screen.

Printing Tools:

Wood scraps, sticks, corrugated rolls and cutouts, erasers, shoe heels, rubber bands, dominoes, cardboard, felt, string, fruits, vegetables, sponges, cord, fabric-covered wire, rubber coasters and stair treads.

Equipment:

Trays, soft-drink cartons, racks or cigar boxes—to hold paint and water jars.

Cans and jars—to hold brushes and to clean brushes.

Boxes—for assorted tools.

Muffin tins, pie plates, jar lids—for color mixing and for distributing paints.

Buckets—for clean or dirty water and for paint rags.

Protective Coatings:

Shellac—soluble in denatured alcohol.

Fixative—soluble in denatured alcohol.

Varnish—soluble in turpentine.

Lacquer—follow directions on the container.

Plastic Spray—follow directions on the container.

Paraffin—to melt and brush on the surface.

Wax—in paste or liquid form; polish the dry wax carefully with a soft cloth or a cleansing tissue.

Talc—to cut the reflective quality of coatings.

Water-soluble paints are usually used for decorating papier-mâché crafts because they are suitable for absorbent paper surfaces, are inexpensive, and can be washed off tools, hands and clothing with soap and water. A wide range of colors, tints and shades can be had by mixing reds, yellows and blues with each other and with black and white.

Remember that colors and color schemes are personal choices. Do not worry about color theories that confuse or prejudice you but explore color mixtures and color use. Discover which colors advance and which seem to recede. Observe how colors are affected by each other or by black and white in mixtures or when one is used next to another. Notice how they are affected by light or shade.

Contrast is important and can be achieved in different ways. Do you recognize light, middle and dark colors? Have you ever lightened a color with water or with white paint to make a tint of that color, and have you mixed a shade by adding black to a color? Value is the quantity of light or dark in a color.

Have you neutralized or grayed a pure color by mixing with it the complementary color? Blue and orange, red and green, yellow and violet complement each other. How much of the complement do you need to mix your favorite grayed color?

In using color, try to make it obey you. Use it to give impressions of softness or hardness, of cold or warmth, of stillness or movement, of

111

dullness or brilliance. Before you paint, close your eyes and imagine the painted craft. Are you sure of the impression you wish to give?

Textures can show different feeling qualities. Texture doodle patches are fun to invent and can show you the difference in smooth and rough impressions.

It is fun to use shapes, colors and textures that are not realistic. Work for pleasing arrangements that fit and suit the surface space. When an arrangement is well planned, it is easy to see; it captures attention and holds it!

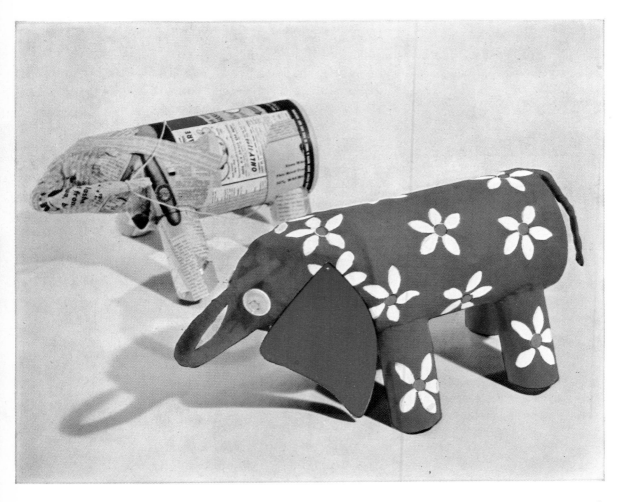

Crafts, courtesy of Binney & Smith Inc.; photograph, courtesy of McCall's Children's Annual, Volume I.

Crafts, courtesy of Binney & Smith Inc.; photograph,
courtesy of McCall's Children's Annual, Volume I.

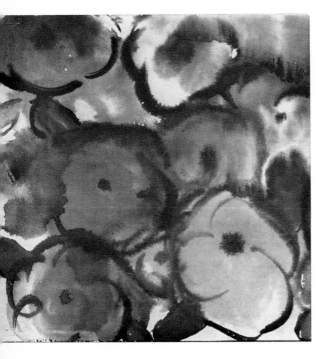

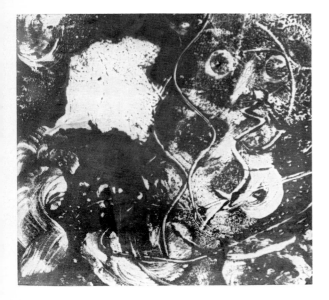

Experiments with Water-soluble Paints

1. Free direct painting with soft or stiff brushes on damp or dry surfaces.

> Can you mix or blend colors on a curved surface?
>
> Do you wash brushes carefully after use?

2. Controlled brush work to fill in lightly sketched areas or for careful line work and details.

> Can you keep adjoining colors from running together?

3. Dry-brush work, with and without stencils.

> Can you use both soft and stiff brushes?
>
> Have you explored different papers for stencils?

4. Spatter work with spray guns or toothbrush and spatula.

> Have you spattered over arrangements of string or cut and torn papers?
>
> Do you prefer to fill in some of the areas recorded by spraying over arrangements?

5. Sponge painting with natural and synthetic sponges.

> Have you cut sponges into different shapes to use as printing tools?
>
> Can you use lightly loaded sponges for stencil repeats?

6. Scratch work on dry tempera with an assortment of scraping tools.

> Have you applied the tempera over a shellacked surface?
>
> Do you need a tempera and soap mixture to cover the shellac?
>
> Have you tried a contrasting paint color under the shellac?

7. Scratch work on wet finger paint using fingernails or scraping tools.

Do you need a shellacked undercoat?

Have you applied finger paint with fingers, brushes and sponges?

Is there contrast of textures in your work?

8. Printing with tools on a painted background.

Have you used contrasting colors?

Can you make new tools by carving an eraser or a vegetable, or by cementing raised materials on a scrap of wood?

9. Screen printing with finger paint.

Have you applied, on an organdy screen, designs created with a heavy coat of wax crayons or thick nail polish?

What household objects of hard rubber can be used as squeegees?

10. Brush lines over solid color areas or over dry brush or printed areas when they are needed to connect the areas.

How do you hold a brush to control or guide it?

What kind of brush do you prefer for precise work?

11. Solid paint areas over line work or texture to provide contrast or catch the eye.

Are some colors more opaque than others?
Do you prefer strong or subtle contrast?

12. Mixtures of water-soluble paints and other materials:

Dry or liquid paint mixed with enough paste, salt, sawdust, cornstarch or plaster of Paris, to make a stiff batter. Use stiff brushes or a spatula to apply it. Incise textures or imbed materials in the moist surface.

Tempera paint mixed with enough gold tempera to produce copper, brass, and other warm metallic colors.

Tempera or water colors applied on dry shellac to provide a crackled look. Add a little liquid soap to the paint to make it adhere to the surface.

Photograph, courtesy of Ruth H. Winship, Springville, New York.

Water colors mixed with white powder paint or white tempera to produce opaque tints.

Mix dry powder paint with colorless varnish and turpentine. Sprinkle sparkle or tiny beads on the moist surface.

Combine water-color washes with pen and ink work on wet or dry paper surfaces.

Exploring Crayons

Materials:

Wax crayons, standard or large sizes—for a sheen, for resist, encaustic or scraping experiments.

Pressed crayons for a dull finish—for fine lines and textures or for crayon overlay.

Mixed Media Experiments:

Tempera paints, water colors, brushes.

Scraping Tools:

Single-edged razor blades, knives, forks, linoleum and wood-carving tools, nail files, pen points, hairpins and hatpins, nails, combs, clay tools, toothpicks, fingernails, notched tin or celluloid.

Encaustic Equipment:

Candles, electric plates and stoves, soldering irons, infrared heat lamps, brushes, palette knives.

Solvents:

Turpentine, banana oil.

Protective Coatings:

Shellac, varnish, lacquer, plastic spray.

Crayons are popular for many reasons. Young children like the many bright and glowing colors available. Older students enjoy new ways of using them. Little time is needed for preparation and cleaning up. Little expense is involved since tools for exploration are found in the home.

Trials can include color blending and mixing with the point or side of an unwrapped crayon, varied strokes with the crayon point and with plain or notched scraps. Practice twists, turns and zigzag motions and different pressures.

If initial explorations are not satisfying, let your curiosity and imagination challenge you to further trials using crayon alone and with other media.

Experiments with Crayons

1. Free direct applications of crayons on a light-colored paper surface. Try line designs, textures, solid spots and a covering coat of blended colors.

2. Crayon work on a tempera painted surface. Let the tempera show through the crayon color or make the crayon work opaque in some areas.

3. Heavy and light applications on printed newspaper.

4. Light or heavy color use on papier-mâché objects which have had a final coat of unprinted newspaper or paper toweling.

5. Heavy wax crayon applied near a stencil edge, moved with a hard eraser to the craft surface. Try brown wrapping paper, construction paper and waxed papers for stencils.

6. Apply flowing washes of tempera or water-color paints over heavy wax crayon lines and small filled-in areas. Select a contrasting color or value for the wash. Try sponging over the crayon with water before adding brushloads of paint.

7. Try various ways of scraping: Cover light and bright wax crayon areas with black or dark-colored crayons. With different tools, scratch and scrape away the dark overcoat to expose lines, textures or patches of the light colors. Or mix liquid soap with dark tempera colors to use as the overcoat. Light tempera colors and soap can be brushed over dark crayons.

8. Encaustic methods vary. They include ways of painting with melted colored wax, and other ways in which heat is used to fuse the colors. Supervision is necessary when candles, soldering irons, heat lamps and stoves are used by children. Make a simple safe heat source by wiring two light bulbs in a small metal plant box and add a wire rack top. Cookie sheets, pie pans and muffin tins can be used for melting the crayon scraps. Add a little hot water to each color to help keep the wax soft or use a little turpentine to thin the color and keep it flexible.

9. Brush or rub turpentine or banana oil over crayon. Gently rub the dry surface with a soft cloth to restore the glow.

10. Use fine sandpaper or talc over heavy applications of wax crayon to dull the finish.

Exploring Trimmings

Trimming materials are valuable only when they help you to convey your meaning. Accents of paper, fabric, yarns, natural materials, metal, glass or plastics are often more effective when their use is limited. Aim for an application that holds attention by considering contrast in size, shape, color and value.

Select the trimming material that appeals to you and work with it to discover its possibilities and its uses. The trimming should not interfere with the intended purpose of the papier-mâché object.

Surface design and color should bring together all the elements which serve the purpose of the craft.

Evaluation

Individuals differ in taste and need time to develop good taste. To grow in ability to design, an evaluation of experiments, based on the level of the individual, is essential. Appreciation and encouragement are necessary to assure confidence.

Perhaps some of these questions will help you to evaluate students' work or your own:

Has there been contact with fine examples?

Is originality shown in ideas, in expression?

Have individual techniques been developed?

Have personality and process been emphasized, rather than the product?

Has the work good proportion of lines, masses, values, colors?

Is there a part that holds the attention?

Does the work express mood or feeling?

Has an impression been expressed simply?

Have the experiences been enjoyable ones?

Exhibits

Exhibits of papier-mâché are one means of gaining appreciation and encouragement. When display space is limited, the exhibit can be changed often to show everyone's work. Students enjoy selecting the examples to show and everyone can cooperate in painting backgrounds, constructing display shelves and in preparing invitations and announcements.

In school buildings—classrooms, hallways, libraries or cafeterias provide possible exhibit space. Special exhibits to loan merchants, churches, social and service organizations and hospitals will develop community interest in creative activities and give pleasure and stimulation to others.

Photograph, *Authenticated News.*

Dance Masks made by native craftsmen of Fort Rupert on Vancouver Island.

Chapter Fifteen

SOURCES AND RESOURCES

Books

Art Activities for the Very Young
F. Louis Hoover
Davis Publications, Inc., 1961
Worcester, Massachusetts

Arts and Crafts for Elementary Teachers
Wankleman, Richards, Wigg
William C. Brown Co., 1954
Dubuque, Iowa

Arts and Crafts in Our Schools
C. D. and Margaret Gaitskell
Charles A. Bennett Co., Inc., 1959
Peoria, Illinois

Art Education for Slow Learners
Charles and Margaret Gaitskell
Charles A. Bennett Co., Inc., 1953
Peoria, Illinois

Art Education in the Kindergarten
Charles and Margaret Gaitskell
Charles A. Bennett Co., Inc., 1958
Peoria, Illinois

Art in the College Program of General Education
Ernest Ziegfeld
Bureau of Publications
Teachers College, Columbia
  University
New York, New York

Art from Scrap
Reed and Orze
Davis Publications, Inc., 1960
Worcester, Massachusetts

Arts of the South Seas
Ralph Linton and Paul Wingert, in collaboration with Rene d'Harnoncourt
The Museum of Modern Art
New York, New York

Art Today
Ray Faulkner, Edwin Ziegfeld,
  Gerald Hill
Henry Holt and Co., rev. 1956
New York, New York

Audio-Visual Methods in Teaching
Edgar Dale
The Dryden Press, rev. 1957
New York, New York

Art Workshop Leaders Planning Guide
Howard Conant
Davis Publications, Inc.
Worcester, Massachusetts

Bulletin Boards and Display
Randall and Haines
Davis Publications, Inc., 1961
Worcester, Massachusetts

Calder
James Johnson Sweeney
Museum of Modern Art, 1951
New York, New York

Children Are Artists
Daniel M. Mendelowitz
Stanford University Press, 1953
Stanford, California

Collage and Construction in Elementary and Junior High Schools
Lois Lord
Davis Publications, Inc., 1958
Worcester, Massachusetts

Creative Expression with Crayons
Elise Reid Boylston
Davis Publications, Inc., 1953
Worcester, Massachusetts

Creative Hands
Cox and Weismann
John Wiley & Sons, 1951
New York, New York

Creative and Mental Growth
Viktor Lowenfeld
Macmillan Co., 1952
New York, New York

Creative Teaching in Art
Victor D'Amico
International Textbook Co., 1953
Scranton, Pennsylvania

Creating a Good Environment for Learning
1954 Yearbook
Association for Supervision and
  Curriculum Development
National Education Association
1201 16th Street, N.W.
Washington 6, D.C.

Creating with Paper
Pauline Johnson
University of Washington Press, 1938
Seattle, Washington

Design, A Creative Approach
Sybil Emerson
International Textbook Co., 1953
Scranton, Pennsylvania

Creative Wood Design
Ernst Rottger
Reinhold Publishing Corp.
New York 22, New York

Discovering Design
Marion Downer
Lothrop, Lee & Shepard Co., 1947
419 Park Avenue, South
New York, New York

Education and Art
Edited by Edwin Ziegfeld
Unesco, 1953
New York, New York

Education and the Nature of Man
Marie I. Rasey and Earl C. Kelley
Harper and Brothers
New York, New York

Education for What Is Real
Earl C. Kelley
Harper & Brothers
New York, New York

Education Through Art
Herbert Read
Pantheon Books, Inc., 1949
New York, New York

Exploring Art
Louise C. Kainz and Olive L. Riley
Harcourt, Brace and World, 1947
New York, New York

Finger Painting, available from libraries
Ruth Faison Shaw
Little, Brown, 1934
Boston, Massachusetts

Photograph, courtesy of Wilma Geer Bradbury, Falmouth Foreside, Maine.

How-To-Do-It Series
Denver Public Schools
Denver, Colorado

How to Make Shapes in Space
Toni Hughes
E. P. Dutton & Co., Inc., 1955
New York, New York

Indian Art of the United States
Frederic H. Douglas and
Rene d'Harnoncourt
The Museum of Modern Art
New York, New York

100 Years of Costume in America
Rose Netzorg Kerr
The Davis Press, Inc., 1951
Worcester, Massachusetts

Knifecraft, booklet
Nik Krevitsky
C. Howard Hunt Pen Co., 1954
Camden, New Jersey

Mask Making, Creative Methods and Techniques
Matthew Baranski
Davis Publications, Inc., 1955
Worcester, Massachusetts

Meaningful Art Education
Mildred M. Landis
Charles A. Bennett, 1951
Peoria, Illinois

Meaning in Crafts
Edward L. Matill
Prentice-Hall, Inc., 1959
Englewood Cliffs, New Jersey

Modelling for Amateurs
Clifford and Rosemary Ellis
The Studio Publications, Inc., 1944
625 Madison Avenue
New York 22, New York

Murals for Schools
Arne W. Randall
Davis Publications, Inc., 1956
Worcester, Massachusetts

Painting and Personality
Rose H. Alschuler and LaBerta
Hattwick
University of Chicago Press, 1947
Chicago, Illinois

Photograph, courtesy of Anthony J. Lauck, C.S.C.,
University of Notre Dame, Notre Dame, Indiana.

Insulating cement used as a sculptural medium.

129

Photograph, courtesy of William E. Reed, Dormont High School, Pittsburgh, Pennsylvania.

130

Painting for Enjoyment
Doris Lee and Arnold Blanch
Tudor Publishing Co., 1947
New York, New York

Paper Sculpture
Grace Johnston
Davis Publications, Inc., 1954
Worcester, Massachusetts

Puppet Theatre Handbook
Marjorie Batchelder
Harper and Brothers, 1947
New York, New York

Science Fun With Milk Cartons
Herman and Nina Schneider
Whittlesey House
McGraw-Hill Book Company, 1953
New York, New York

Teaching Art in the Elementary School
Margaret Erdt
Rinehart and Co., 1954
New York, New York

Teaching Art to Children
Blanche Jefferson
Allyn and Bacon, Inc., 1959
Boston, Massachusetts

Tempera Painting
Zolton Sepesky
Studio Books, Inc., 1951
New York—London

The Artist in Each of Us
Florence Cane
Pantheon Books, Inc., 1951
New York, New York

The Arts in the Classroom
Natalie R. Cole
The John Day Co., 1942
New York, New York

The Eagle, the Jaguar, and the Serpent: Indian Art of the Americas
Miguel Covarrubias
Alfred A. Knopf, 1954
New York, New York

The First Book of Dolls
Helen Hoke
Franklin Watts, Inc., 1954
575 Lexington Avenue
New York 22, New York

The First Book of Puppets
Mortiz Jagendorf
Franklin Watts, Inc., 1952
New York, New York

The Language of Vision
Gyorgy Kepes
Paul Theobald, 1945
Chicago, Illinois

The Nature of Creative Activity
Viktor Lowenfeld
Harcourt, Brace & World, Inc., 1939
New York, New York

The New Vision
Lazlo Moholy-Nagy
George Wittenborn Inc., 1947
New York, New York

The Unfolding of Artistic Activity: Its Basis, Processes and Implications
Henry Schaeffer-Simmern
University of California Press, 1948
Berkeley, California

This Is Art Education: Series
Teachers College, Columbia University
Columbia University Press
New York, New York

This Is Teaching
Marie I. Rasey
Harper and Brothers, 1950
New York, New York

The Workshop Way of Learning
Earl C. Kelley
Harper and Brothers, 1951
New York, New York

Vision in Motion
Laszlo Moholy-Nagy
Paul Theobald, 1947
Chicago, Illinois

Water Color Painting
Adolf Dehn
Studio Publications, 1954
New York, New York

Ways with Water Color
Ted Kautzky, N.A.
Reinhold Publishing Corp., 1949
New York, New York

What People Wore
Douglas Gorsline
Viking Press, 1952
New York, New York

Your Child and His Art
Viktor Lowenfeld
Macmillan Co., 1953
New York, New York

Magazines

American Artist
111 Fourth Avenue
New York 3, New York

Arts & Activities
8150 N. Central Park Avenue
Skokie, Illinois

Craft Horizons
601 Fifth Avenue
New York 17, New York

Design
337 South High Street
Columbus 15, Ohio

Interiors
Whitney Publications, Inc.
New York, New York

School Arts
Davis Publications, Inc.
44 Portland Street
Worcester 8, Massachusetts

Films and Directories

A Directory of 2660-16mm. Film Libraries Bulletin 1953, No. 7
U.S. Dept. of Health, Education and Welfare
Office of Education
Washington, D.C.

Alexander Calder: Sculpture and Constructions–Rental
The Museum of Modern Art Film Library
New York, New York

Animules—Rental
International Film Bureau
332 S. Michigan Avenue
Chicago 4, Illinois

Arts and Crafts of the Southwest Indians—Free
The Atchison, Topeka & Santa Fe Railroad
120 Broadway
New York, New York

Art for the Family: Kinescope Series—Rental
Family Portrait
City Inspired
Up in the Sky
Under the Sea
In Touch with Your World
Museum of Modern Art Film Library
New York, New York

Art of the Pacific Northwest—Rental
Cinevision, Inc.
49 West 19th Street
New York 11, New York

Bailey Films, Inc.—Rental
6509 De Longpre Avenue
Hollywood 28, New York

How to Make a Puppet

How to Make a Mask

How to Make Papier-Mâché Animals

Exploring in Paint

Torn Paper

Crayon Resist

Children Are Creative

Films on Art
Edited by William McK. Chapman
The American Federation of Arts, 1952
1083 Fifth Avenue
New York 28, New York

Loon's Necklace—Rental
Encyclopedia Britannica Films, Inc.
1150 Wilmette Avenue
Wilmette, Illinois

Pre-Columbian Mexican Art— Rental
Brandon Films, Inc.
200 West 57th Street
New York, New York

Puppetry: String Marionettes

Encyclopedia Britannica Films, Inc.
Wilmette, Illinois

Making a Mask—Rental

Creative Hands, Series 11
International Film Bureau
Chicago, Illinois

Through the Enchanted Gate:
Kinescope Series—10 films—
Rental

The Museum of Modern Art Film
Library
11 West 53rd Street
New York 19, New York

Works of Calder—Rental

Museum of Modern Art Film
Library
New York, New York

For catalogues, please write to the
film distributors already listed, and
to the following:

Cinema 16, Inc.
175 Lexington Avenue
New York 16, New York

Contemporary Films
267 West 25th Street
New York, New York

Film Center, Inc.
20 E. Huron Street
Chicago, Illinois

Film Images, Inc., A.F. Films
1860 Broadway
New York, New York

Films of the Nations
62 West 45th Street
New York, New York

Indian ceremonial masks from the "Loon's Necklace."   Photograph, courtesy of Encyclopedia Britannica Films, Inc.

133

National Film Board of Canada
680 Fifth Avenue
New York 19, New York

United Nations Films
The United Nations
New York, New York

Television

A Television Policy for Education, 1952

Edited by Carroll V. Newsom
American Council on Education
Washington, D.C.

Children and TV—Making the Most of It

Association for Childhood Education
International
3615 Wisconsin Avenue, N.W.
Washington 16, D.C.

How to Use TV: In School and in Home

Metropolitan School Study Council
525 West 120th Street
New York 27, New York

Joint Committee on Educational Television, 1951

1785 Massachusetts Avenue, N.W.
Washington 6, D.C.

National Association of Radio and Television Broadcasters

The Television Code, effective
March, 1952
1771 N. Street, N.W.
Washington 6, D.C.

TV Bibliography, 1954

TV Committee
Committee on Art Education
Museum of Modern Art
New York, New York

Television and Education in the United States, 1952

Charles A. Siepmann
Unesco
New York, New York

Television in Our Schools

Bulletin 1952, No. 16, Government
Printing Office
U.S. Office of Education
Department of Health, Education
and Welfare
Washington 25, D.C.

Music

Songs Children Like—Folk Songs from Many Lands

Association for Childhood Education
International
3615 Wisconsin Avenue, N.W.
Washington 16, D.C.

Songs, Rhythms, Instrumental Records for Elementary Grades

Educational Department
Radio Corporation of America
R.C.A. Victor Division
Camden, New Jersey

Book-of-the-Month Club, Inc.

Children's Record Division
345 Hudson Street
New York 14, New York

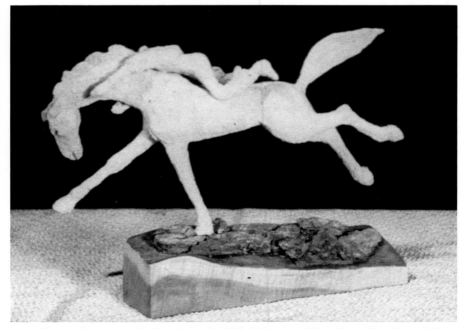

Photograph, courtesy of Anthony J. Lauck, C.S.C., University of Notre Dame, Notre Dame, Indiana.
Insulating cement used as a sculptural medium.